Cal Sacks

Yellowstone

Yellowst

PHOTOGRAPHS BY CHARLES STEINHACKER AND OTHERS

A Chanticleer Press Edition

one
a century of the wilderness idea

Ann and Myron Sutton

THE MACMILLAN COMPANY, NEW YORK
COLLIER-MACMILLAN LTD., LONDON
AND
YELLOWSTONE LIBRARY AND
MUSEUM ASSOCIATION

In appreciation of Hugh D. Galusha, Jr.
for his devotion to the National Park Idea,
for his leadership of the Yellowstone Library and Museum Association,
and for the inspiration he gave to so many.

The Macmillan Company, New York, New York Collier-Macmillan Canada Ltd., Toronto, Ontario

Planned and produced by Chanticleer Press, New York

Printed by Amilcare Pizzi, S.p.A., Milan, Italy

Library of Congress Catalog Card Number 72–183207. Published in 1972

Contents

A MESSAGE FROM H.R.H. PRINCE PHILIP

To anyone concerned about the conservation of nature the very name of Yellowstone is like a battle cry. This is where it all started; Yellowstone was the first wilderness set aside for a national park, and it remains an inspiration and the confirmation that dreams can be made to come true.

Many people all over the world are now working on similar dreams and I think they could not do better than to paste up over their desks the word "Yellowstone." Just looking up at it should help them to overcome those only too frequent moments of black depression when the difficulties seem hopeless, enthusiasm evaporated, and the pressure of other problems seems threatening to any progress.

These difficulties and problems are very real. It may come as a nasty jolt to cherished ideals to find that there are whole groups of people whose self-interest makes them oppose any idea of a national park. When so much seems obvious to the dedicated naturalist it comes as an unpleasant reminder of reality to have to deal with poachers, commercial exploiters, racketeers, not to speak of landholders tenacious of their property. Meanwhile, hanging like a threatening cloud over all plans and projects is the problem of cost. This would be bad enough by itself but when it is sometimes coupled with idleness, inefficiency and waste, it needs the inspiration of Yellowstone to restore the will to go on.

Yet go on we must. Every year it becomes more obvious that if we humans are to allow the wilderness and its inhabitants to survive we must set aside areas—big areas—for their exclusive use. Where a clash of interest occurs, and it will occur even more frequently as the world's human population increases, we must simply harden our hearts and remind ourselves that because of our power we have a responsibility for all life on earth.

Foreword

Primitive man did quite a good job empirically in caring for his environment. Of course he had little or no conscious notion of looking after his country. There was so much of it and only a few men. Such change as he did bring about often produced variety which led to ultimate enrichment of flora and fauna. There was, also, a natural prudence in primitive man; an animal killed provided so much more than food: there was bone, horn, hide and sinews, all to be used as valuable contributions to a gradually improving standard of living.

There have been primitive men into our own time, and a hundred years ago there were some in the area of Yellowstone Park. Had so-called civilized man not looked in, the Yellowstone would not have become what it is now, a great window on a panorama of nature and an educational institution for the whole world as well as the nation; nor would it have presented the continuous problems of management with which the U. S. National Park Service is faced today.

In the barest terms, here was a high country with a hard winter climate, carrying fair numbers of hoofed animals and their predators, but a remarkably small population of human beings, who were self-reliant, self-sustaining. The present picture is of a summer influx of over two million people, who need rapid ingress and egress and want to be moderately comfortable for the few nights they are in this primeval area of wildest nature.

The last hundred years has been the period of learning what the idea of a national park really means. It has been a shriving experience. There was the initial idea, bold and forward thinking in a time when it was taken for granted that any natural resources were to be exploited for human profit. But how do you implement the idea of a national park in practice? This was the idealistic problem which the nation faced altruistically.

In earlier years predatory animals such as wolves and mountain lions were hunted almost to extinction. Now the predators are being coaxed back to help do a job civilized man has not fully managed to do—the control of the elk herds to numbers within the carrying capacity of the country. The Yellowstone sanctuary has helped materially to make the future of the trumpeter swan reasonably safe, and the Yellowstone herd of bison is a magnificent spectacle.

Rangers in the Yellowstone were always dedicated men and it is with their skill and knowledge that the communication system has been devised so that as little damage as possible has been done in getting people to and from the park. The first Director of the National Park Service, Stephen Mather, set an example of dedication by his own tireless ranging of the Yellowstone on horseback.

Management remains the keynote, of plants and animals and men, humane management without any sectional bias. In a world where we have had so much destruction of natural resources and pollution of air, water and soil, the United States has established an ethos of conservation of which the national park idea is a spearhead. Yellowstone is an earnest for the future.

FRANK FRASER DARLING

1

Into the Wilderness

I can conceive of no more wonderful and attractive region for the explorer.

FERDINAND V. HAYDEN, 1872

August 14. The temperature is below freezing again. Along the edge of the lake and in the meadows there are crystals of frost on the leaves. Our breath turns into steam as we strap on packs and prepare to depart for a week's trip through the Thorofare country, in the southeast corner of Yellowstone National Park. The first rays of the sun strike the crystals of frost and change them into droplets that cling to the blades of grass like strings of jewels. As we mount our horses and set off up the trail, we button our jackets against the chill.

It is obvious that we are entering a land where human beings are intruders. There are no roads, no stores, no houses on this part of the Yellowstone River. This is the domain of moose and grizzly bears and a host of other wild animals, and we do not intend to remain, or to disturb what we find. We have kept our group as small as possible. In reality, we are not a party of five, but five parties of one. Each enters the Thorofare for a different reason. Each has his own desires, his own experiences, his own reactions to the high-country wilderness.

The trail ahead is a public trail. Anyone can take it. The prospect that we may encounter other people does not disturb us. Nor does it matter that Yellowstone, or in fact all of Wyoming, has been explored. The footsteps of the early explorers sound only in memory. Our trip is as much a voyage of discovery as theirs was. Whoever we meet will probably have the same aims as we: to breathe the sharp scented mountain air, to feel the joy of a clean, pure, unfamiliar world, to lose all sense of time and urgency, to hear the music, to forget—for a few days simply to start life anew and live it differently.

You cannot tell what each member of our little party is thinking. Each is preoccupied with looking around him, and there is little evidence of his innermost thoughts. Perhaps one sees each scene with an artist's mind and eye, and may someday put it on canvas. Another sees every vista as though through a camera lens, and can record each image forever as remembered now. Another's eyes are botanist's, rang-

Sunrise and morning mist, Yellowstone River.

ing from flower to flower and leaf to leaf, categorizing a few according to family. We share this journey as friends, but no two of us will have the same experience.

Long, tree-laden ridges form the western edge of the Yellowstone River valley. From the south these ridges emerge from nowhere, the "nowhere" of the Thorofare country, and end as bluffs above the waters of Yellowstone Lake. The river meanders for miles through meadows of its own making and reaches far back into the wild country, creating a basin so long and wide that we cannot view it all from the trail.

Young lodgepole pines surround us and at times seem to enclose the trail in a tunnel. Their branches come out of the shadows as though to clutch at one another, while the uppermost limbs push their needled clusters into the widening, warming rays of the sun.

We loosen our jackets a little. Not a breeze yet freshens the woods. The stalks of lilies, so slender and fragile, stand still; a sun's ray lodges in one of the blossoms for a moment, then seems to burst out from it. Discovering each tulip-shaped flower to have a patch of purple and green in the center of ivory-white petals, we identify it as mariposa lily.

Monkshood stands hip-high beside the trail. Harebells spread out like waves of blue. The shadows are spotted with yarrow, aster, fireweed, buckwheat, lupine. . . . Our eyes rove everywhere at once—up and down, far and near, right, left, ahead, behind—but we are no match for the mountain wilderness. Had we a hundred eyes and a score of minds on which to imprint all these images, it would not be sufficient.

The mosquitoes have diminished a trifle, but enough remain to make any stop in the shade unwise. As the sun climbs higher over peaks in the Absaroka Range, the warm air wakens more winged creatures than we can count: deer flies, horseflies, houseflies, hornets. Insects gather on cinquefoil flowers. Butterflies light on yarrow. And as for species that inhabit the grass or the forest floor, we haven't even time to begin a study of them.

Today we must cover sixteen miles, tomorrow another sixteen, and so on. This is disturbing; it is much too fast. We are anxious to tarry and stop, but cannot as often as we'd like. The horses make too much clatter. We resolve to send them ahead and get off and walk as often as possible.

The morning passes. Shadows brighten. Glooms turn into soft-lit glades of moss and huckleberry. Downed trees lie where felled—by wind, by age, by lightning—and no one clears them away. Indeed, the forest itself relaxes in a state of ecological repose, as in a national park it should. This is not a sleepy repose, despite the quiet that often gives us that impression. We sense and see a great deal going on—the fragrance of decay, the vigorous growth (with young trees springing up in nearly all locations), the bustle of birds and squirrels and chipmunks, the hints of worlds we scarcely see.

Had this region not been set aside as a public park a century ago, we would now see a different world: summer homes, perhaps, on the ridges above, gasoline stations through the trees, cattle or sheep on the meadows. . . . None of that is here, nor will be. Yellowstone is not only a geographic entity but a place where an idea is being tested. It is a strange idea and almost, one would think, anathema to man. For once in his long and violent evolution he has taken an exceptionally rich and beautiful portion of his surroundings and decided to leave it almost entirely alone. The idea seems to be an immensely promising but fragile one: man ordered himself not to shoot any animals, cut any trees, pollute any waters, or otherwise disrupt the wilderness that he had been eradicating methodically for millenniums elsewhere. So far, though at considerable peril, the idea has worked —and our ride is not far different from those of the early explorers who first came through here a century and a half ago.

Land of Moose and Meadows

The Yellowstone River, for most of the way, is hidden beyond head-high willow thickets. Now and then a gull flies up from it, or a duck, or a kingfisher; and redwings sing in the marshes. All life seems to respond to the rapid warming so characteristic of western mornings. We soon remove our jackets and stow them in packs or tie them about our waists.

Around a bend in the trail we suddenly find ourselves at the edge of the river, and almost as suddenly we see the moose—two of them. They are as still as statues, a male and a female, standing knee-deep in a channel partly obscured by a small peninsula of woods. Their stance and their size—seven and a half feet high at the shoulders and weighing a thousand pounds or so—give them unmistakable command of the environment; while wary of men and wolves, they are capable of stamping either into the dust. Here, however, the moose has not been conditioned to fear the depredations of men. These two do not give ground. They stand and watch, and as we continue their only movement is an almost imperceptible swivel of their massive necks as their eyes keep us in focus.

Lunch only whets our appetite for more of the seen and unseen. As we sit by Monument Creek we begin to realize the considerable display of color in this wilderness. Beneath the rippling waters of the stream lie igneous pebbles and boulders of yellow, orange, gray, green, red, and purple. A little while later, riding across the meadows, we come to colors of a different kind, the living colors of wild flowers. These at first seem out of place in a land so brutally frozen in winter. But during the scant three months of summer the plants carry on their age-old, annual spectacle of perpetuating the species. So densely grow the grasses, sedges, strawberries, gentians, larkspurs, clovers, monkshoods, asters, dandelions, and dozens of other species, that we seldom see the ground or the smaller animals that live among the grasses. When we near the lowlands, with their wetness and nourishing soil, the willows become head-high and we almost disappear. It is as though this great biomass absorbed the energy from sunlight and literally exploded with life.

Not long after leaving the luncheon site, we break out of the woods into one of the widest of meadows, a slowly descending swale that merges with willows at least a mile away. Everything to be seen, each valley and mountain range, the lake, the river, the meadows, every tree in the forest, is in its original state, unmodified by men. The air is so clean and pure that it magnifies the mountains and makes them seem much closer than they are. But the distances are great indeed. We look east across eight miles of open air to the summits of the Absaroka Range, west twenty miles to Mount Sheridan, and northwest sixty miles to the Gallatin Range. It is a big country that belongs to no one, yet belongs to all.

"Enjoy" is the word for this afternoon, a hundred kinds of enjoyment. If a sculptor were along he would have a field day: gnarled roots and trunks on the forest floor; cracks and twistings of naked stumps deceased and debarked; rolling, convoluted patterns of aging limbs. We stop and investigate engravings made by beetles on the lodgepole logs. The wood, now bleached, has been gouged out and channeled in designs so intricate they can hardly be retraced. There is a simple artistry about this free-flow form, and it captures the imagination. The creatures whose paths crossed here were of a system of life completely different from our own, yet linked to it.

The farther we go into the interior, the richer the ecosystem seems to become. Patches of monkshood and lily increase in size and density of stems. Cow parsnips reach a height of six or seven feet. Blueberry grows in thickets. Alders enclose the streams. Mosses clothe the rocks. Lichens festoon the branches of trees and occasionally glow with a brilliant chartreuse when touched by a spot of sunlight. Wherever this happens, color radiates far out of proportion to the size of the lichen tufts; it pigments the shadows, erases the gloom, and renders the forest a veritable gallery of impressionistic art.

There is a wild array of color. In the meadows, fruiting tips of grasses have a purplish tone. Abundant blues of gentian, lupine, and larkspur line the trail,

Overleaf: Cow elk and a group of young elk among Everts' thistles.

as do the purples of monkshood and harebell, the magenta of fireweed, the scarlet of paintbrush, and the yellow of mushrooms and sunflowers. Red-cap lichens and red-berried kinnikinnick command the forest floor. There are acres of lilies, mingling with sagebrush and looking from afar like so many balls of cotton. Rich deep reds adorn the meadows where leaves such as those of wild geranium have already turned to their autumn color. Old needles on the pines are orange, the distant slopes of Mount Sheridan are orange, and over all is a sky so blue as to seem unreal.

A grouse ambles casually aside as we pass, continuing to feed a few feet off the trail. A sparrow hops alongside, and at first we think it is a female feigning injury. Not this time—the bird is after insects which our passage has caused to fly.

Another meadow. It is hard to imagine the existence of this much open space, unspoiled, on land. The grass is unbroken for miles, swept by the wind like waves at sea, the surface altered only by copses of cinquefoil. The light and heat of the sun pour uninterruptedly out of the sky to sear our hands and arms and faces. The temperature in the shade is 78° F., but direct sunlight on the meadows dries out and draws the skin as tight as a drum. For hours, even as it falls toward the western ridge, the sun sustains this intensity, and only where the path enters woods do we find relief.

The trail soon brings us to the Yellowstone River again, and for half an hour we relax on the bank of the stream. The world seems not to be moving; all time appears stationary, and if there were things we ought to have done before leaving, we now begin to forget what they were. A voice seems to say: "Slow down and live!"

So we do. For minutes we look at the river, nothing more. It rolls on tirelessly, and if we catch the light just right on the rippling water we get the impression of a thousand suns exploding. A raven perched on an old dead snag across the water relaxes, too, although the spotted sandpiper never seems to cease its search along the river's edge. Our ears absorb the soft sounds of the solitude and after a while we lie on our backs in the grass to watch the white clouds drifting by. . . .

On arrival at camp we are tired, dusty, thirsty, hungry, hot, sore, and soaked with perspiration. Wilderness travel is painful and dirty. We are burned and parched, wanting nothing more than to collapse in a heap and stay that way until morning, though the mosquitoes do not allow it. The inner soul, unaffected by physical punishment, is alive and well, however. Our minds try to assemble in order the scenes observed in the past few hours, and at the same time take in the radiant evening glow that bathes the meadows, the woods, the peaks, the clouds. It is no use. We concentrate on the present moment only, and when the color has gone we take off our packs and descend to Thorofare Creek, a small meadow stream. We drink a few cups of icy water, savoring each one slowly, and almost at once are revived.

Wild Gardens

August 15. This morning we arise to a temperature of thirty degrees and wash off lightly in Thorofare Creek, which is akin to brushing the face with ice. Frost covers nearly all of the open meadow and coats the cinquefoil, grass, and willow with odd-shaped crystals of ice. It is a tiny touch of winter that reminds us how short summer really is at this latitude. In less time than we think, autumn will have come and gone, the ground will be coated with snow, and the whole landscape will be buried in white for perhaps six months.

The only visitors then, for the most part, will be rangers, to whom Yellowstone is best when chilled. They come in on ski patrols even when the temperature is 30° or more below zero and visibility limited by a raging blizzard to less than ten feet. If the snow crusts over or sticks to their skis, they sometimes have to break their way for miles, or struggle through slushy snow. Or perhaps by some rare accident they crash through ice on crossing a stream and sink in the freezing water. Yet they are the muscle behind the national park idea. Without their inspections, their repairs, their overall supervision, their endurance of severe conditions, we would hardly enjoy as much freedom and silence as we do on this frosty meadow at dawn.

The ice evaporates as the sun comes over the ridge to the east. We head to the west and cross the Yellowstone River at a shallow ford. Some of the banks of the river downstream have slid into the water, and all that remains after currents have washed away the soil are clusters of pink and white roots on the bottom of the stream, clearly visible at ten feet deep.

We are stiff and sore. Our muscles do not respond with precision to the morning's commands. With little chance to bathe last night, we feel dusty and dried out, skinned, and burned; the insect bites and minor scratches are irritating; on the whole, there is enough to complain about. Yet no one has the slightest intention of turning back. The compensations are overwhelming: no alien noises; no radios; no newspapers; no schedules to keep—only bright sunshine and clear air, mountains, forests, meadows, and streams, in a splendid arrangement. "It would be difficult," wrote the explorer Ferdinand V. Hayden in 1871, "to find a valley in the West that presents as fine a picture to the eye."

Our plan is to travel through one of the most remote parts of the region today, heading west along the boundary between Yellowstone National Park and the Teton Wilderness Area, crossing the Two Ocean Plateau, and proceeding down the Snake River drainage.

In attempting to find Lynx Creek we lose our way. With so much to observe, we are less attentive to where we are going than to what we are seeing, and for a few joyous minutes we haven't the slightest idea where we are or which way to go. In efforts to relocate the trail, we pass and repass a thicket in which a cow moose stands quietly. She does not move; she may have a calf nearby. We keep our distance.

After finding Lynx Creek and starting up it, we enter a forest more luxuriant than we had imagined could grow in a region where temperatures vary from 66° below zero to 98° above. Within these extremes the plant life and its associated animals have evolved into varied communities, distinct but all related. Along the banks of Lynx Creek and its tributaries, the vegetation is so dense that it reminds us of a tropical rain forest—with one big difference, the massive display of color.

Arnica and senecio sprinkle the coves with yellow, and there are red and white stalks of coralroot beside the trail. Columbines suspend their ivory-yellow flowers in the shadows. Spring after spring, jingling with the music of falling water, is spotted by the scarlet of paintbrush. Cow parsnip leans over the water, and on the lower slopes are sedge and meadow rue. Scouring rush, one of the most primitive plants in this ecosystem, gathers in masses; its foliage is feathery and its pigments so bright that they give the impression of green fountains showering over the vales. Among the mossy banks are mountain bluebells. The mimulus, or monkeyflower, of the snapdragon family, lifts its bright pink flower trumpets to the sky.

The streams are lined with multiple species of flowers, as profuse and varied as in English country gardens. Purple, yellow, white, and blue predominate. Well could these headwaters of the Yellowstone be called the "rainbow streams." There are so many species that only a competent botanist would know them all.

The whole effect is stunning; it has taken a day to rub out the blots of civilization and synchronize with the wilderness. Now that we have done it we are receptive, sensitive, quick to see the simple elegance of a leaf or a patch of lichen or a rock or a cloud. Two days ago we might have blindly passed such scenes in our car, hurrying on to a destination then considered very important. Now we stop and absorb the fundamentals of the forest, of life itself, of a world in which we biological organisms evolved. In the swift, full life we lead in cities there are never moments

Above: The climbing vines of clematis, in the buttercup family, ornament tree trunks, limbs and rocks in the deeper, moister parts of the forest. *Right*: Glacier lilies bloom even before the snows have melted. At the highest elevations their flowering season may extend into August.

During summer the moose frequents marshes, meadows and willow thickets. In winter its long legs help in traversing deep snow.

enough to contemplate such things as the sheen of silver on a tumbling brook.

Climbing over Two Ocean Pass, we move among groves of alpine fir and meet the flowers of spring still blooming, which raises the question of whether, in these lofty regions, summer comes at all. After noon we stop at Mariposa Lake, a broad sedge basin with shallow waters that harbor a good supply of cutthroat trout. The slopes descending to it are purpled by thousands of monkshood, growing in a fringe of royal velvet. Gnats and flies by the cloud surround us and jays come to investigate our intrusion.

The trail leads on along Mariposa Creek, downhill through more miles of country gardens. Obviously this luxuriant growth must die or diminish in the fall, but come next spring, as it has for centuries, the ponderous mass of life will burgeon again. Would that we could witness the grand, refreshing renewal of it.

Big Game Ridge

August 16.   We awake to find the meadows again encrusted with frost. The grass appears to be adorned with thousands of stars, and every cinquefoil leaf looks as though a shower of diamonds had been sprinkled on it overnight. On capturing the light of the sun, each crystal emits a spectrum of color, and even though the heat soon converts them into droplets of water, they continue to exhibit a field of prisms. By moving his head very slowly an observer may create a play of colors in the field. One drop turns to a brilliant blue. Another yellow. Another orange. Another green.

As we walk through this prismatic meadow, our boots knock loose the glaze of frost in small white showers. At the same time we enjoy some other advantages of prowling at dawn—the cool fresh air, the silence, the greater chance of seeing birds and mammals at their morning feeding.

Before long we are on our way again, across the Snake River, westward and upward to Big Game Ridge. The air becomes thinner and cooler the higher we rise. Moisture decreases, as does the density of the forest. Lodgepoles give way to spruce and fir, except that an old lodgepole here and there stands apart from the others, struggling against the greater severity of the elements at this elevation.

Up here the whitebark pine becomes more common, its light gray bark contrasting with the dark trunks of the young lodgepoles below. Hardy and vigorous whitebarks thrive at high elevations in the West—no pine grows higher here in the Yellowstone country—and they are with us all the way up to the top of Big Game Ridge, more than 10,000 feet above sea level.

We now begin to grasp a little of the complexity of this environment, or at least enough to wonder about a few of the things we see: why whitebark pines predominate here, why meadows have no trees, why ponderosa pines are absent here when they occur so abundantly elsewhere in the West.

The wind comes up with gale force, and we lower our heads against it. On come the jackets, for the wind is cold. Still clinging to the summits are patches of snow, gleaming pink and white in the sun. The pink, another miracle of the high country, is red algae, growing right in the snow and harboring other organisms that are adapted to life amid melting ice.

The terrain becomes rocky, and there is loosened, powdery soil in which pocket gophers have built their elongated mounds. Although the firs, with sharp-pointed tips, lined the lower ridges like teeth on a saw, there are few left at this elevation, and those hardy enough to remain are stunted and twisted. The forest becomes almost exclusively whitebark pine. And as we continue climbing, even that grows scarce.

As usual, tundra vegetation splashes the summits with color. Lupine pours down into ravines as though some hand had upset a giant bottle of ink and washed the slopes in cerulean blue. Elsewhere, phlox and bistort grow among the ice-cracked rocks. And then at last we are on the top, in full command of one of the finest views in Yellowstone National Park.

The land is blue and green—the dark blue of lakes

Left: In the tumbling musical waters of Yellowstone live invertebrates on which certain fish and birds depend for sustenance. *Above*: The water ouzel spends its life beside—or sometimes in—a rushing mountain stream, pursuing aquatic insects.

that fill the basins, partly hidden by hills or promontories, and the green of forests that blanket all but the lakes and meadows. The whole park lies at our feet, so vast (3,472 square miles) that the tips of peaks beyond show only as distant summits in the noonday haze. All roads, all trails, even the thirty or forty thousand people visiting the park today, are engulfed in this great immensity and silence.

Rising thirty miles to the south is the Teton Range, and beyond that, mountains that look to be twice as far away. Below, at a distance of about three miles, are some fifty elk at the edge of a meadow. Other animals, such as bighorns, deer, bears, and foxes, occupy this ridge, but we do not see them. We dismount and send the horses ahead in order to proceed on our own and get much closer to the life of the mountains.

The trail down from Big Game Ridge is steep. At first our boots pound the dry white soil, then sink into mossy earth as the trail once again enters luxuriant forest. The hours we take to hike down Harebell Creek, delaying our progress as often as prudent, are hours of kaleidoscopic color. Each passing image seems better than the last, until our powers to comprehend and retain are exceeded by the volume of sights and sounds. The forest becomes a montage of changing, dissolving images: matronlike fir trees circled with young; Oregon juncos flying to thickets; winds singing gentle notes as they filter through needles of whitebark pine; clusters of delicate forget-me-nots that resemble blue lace; fresh tracks of deer and elk; hawks sailing over; trees scraping together and filling the woods with sounds like those of cellos and violins.

Harebell Creek, a steep-plunging, musical, dancing thread of water, is thwarted by logs behind which gravel deposits have built up terraces. The result is an abundance of waterfalls. Suddenly we are stopped in our tracks by the sight of a strange bird dipping up and down on an old log near some rapids. It moves about in short hops, and remains restless and searching until it spies an insect. There is a quick leap, a

flick of the head, and a jab of the beak. The meal is over. The bird stops for a drink and then, without hesitation, walks right into the little pool at the base of the fall. It enters head first, and completely disappears. It is gone for a time, then emerges and flits from rock to rock before flying to the next lower pool and settling squarely into the midst of the water again. Moments later it surfaces, ruffles its feathers, and flies on down the creek, leaving a musical note that echoes like a bell in the little dell. Few birds are as adapted to life around water as the dipper, or water ouzel. The pools and rapids hold abundant aquatic food, and here the ouzel spends its life. It even suspends its mossy nest beside a splashing fall, which keeps the nest in a constant state of dampness, and there the young are born into a vigorous life of leaping spray and falling water.

When next we see the ouzel it is perched ashore, standing on one foot, asleep.

Time is a needless tool to the ouzel—and to us. The sun is the only clock we want. If we carry a watch and look at it now and then, the hour seems always painfully later than we wish. We are in conflict again: there is distance to travel and too much that we want to stop and see. Tonight we shall sleep very deeply indeed, and tomorrow begin anew.

On the Trail to Heart Lake

August 17. All is not well in this wilderness. Yesterday the primeval quiet was shattered fifteen times with the sound of aircraft and the sight of private and commercial planes flying low overhead. Already it begins this morning—an alien sound in a national park, the kind of thing we came to avoid. Still, we are no longer in social custody. For days we have had no newspapers or news of the outside world, and feel absolutely glad about it. We are still sore and dirty, but that no longer matters. The exhilaration in our minds, the feasts before our eyes, the fragrances, the wind in our faces—all senses are alive.

We cross the Snake River, where a mallard swoops off the water and flies overhead with rapid wing beats. Not far beyond, the path leads into giant meadows on which the yampa, a member of the parsley family, spreads its mass of white flowers as far as the eye can see. In places the grass is compressed, as though an elk or deer or bear had spent the night there. Above, in that clear and dark blue sky, swallows hold conventions among the lodgepole pines that stand out in the open fields like lonesome sentinels.

Nearly an hour is required to cross the major meadows, after which we enter a youthful lodgepole forest. Among the trees are logs in an advanced state of decay, lying scattered and crossed, making X's, crosses, or diamond-shaped enclosures, no doubt marking the site of an old forest fire. A few moments later, a four-point buck mule deer leaps across a vale and into the forest on the opposite side of the valley.

For hours we ride, and Mount Sheridan rises higher before us. During lunch at Sheridan Lake, the wind blows a gale. We rest on a thick grass pallet, watching ducks on the water and moose on the mountain slopes across the lake.

Proceeding around the east face of the mountain, we come to Heart Lake, its deep blue surface roiling with waves and spray. Two marmots screech in warning and tumble down the rocky, grassy slope to their holes. A half mile farther on we reach some open inclines where an avalanche roared in the winter of 1968. It is hard to calculate how many thousands or millions of tons of snow came down the mountain. The thundering mass took tall trees out by the roots and broke them off as though they were so many sticks. The trees were tumbled and jumbled, launched like lances into the surrounding forest, piled like cordwood tossed from the sawyer's bench, or swept down to the edge of the lake—and into it. Rangers coming in the following spring found Heart Lake's surface abundant with floating logs.

Beyond, the colonnaded fir forest is quiet and peaceful, sheltered from winds that race across the lake. Here sun flecks fall on the moss or soften the shadows; Arcadian groves were never fairer. Chickadees chatter in the woods and we arrive at camp accompanied by two kingfishers that take up positions on a limb at the edge of the lake.

We are tired, but it would not be obvious to anyone else. We live each hour for its passing joys, and almost furiously, for the days will end too soon. The members of the party spread out—to the lake, the creek, the forest.

Suddenly through the woods we see a wisp of what appears pure white smoke curling up above the trees. Our first thought is of a forest fire commencing, or a camper's fire where it shouldn't be. Then the white expands into a cloud and shortly afterward evaporates. It is not smoke but a steam cloud, rising in the afternoon sun. We make our way there as rapidly as possible, through hip-high grass, over small rivulets, across mud flats, and arrive in an open vale that is floored with soft white rock. Along the gentle slope is a collection of pools: broad ones of an emerald hue where swirling steam is pushed by gusts of wind, small ones that are muddy, round ones, square ones, odd-shaped ones; some quiet, some boiling.

Beside a larger pool our attention is drawn to yellowish siliceous rock in a pattern of pearls and popcorn. This, as we watch, is slowly immersed when water within the spring overflows. We step as close as we dare for a look at the deposits around the rim, when instantly there is an explosive swish and the air is filled with shooting, steaming, boiling water.

We leap out of the way. For several minutes the waters, hissing and splashing, burst from the pool. At the top of their arcs the droplets catch the yellow rays of the sun and become so many diamonds hurled into the deep blue sky. Our eyes cannot move fast enough to keep up with the action, and the eruption soon subsides. We resolve to wait for another.

Twenty-five minutes later the pool erupts again. Several times we watch, until Rustic Geyser, as it is called on the map, is enveloped by shade. Between eruptions we follow the overflow stream that makes its way down the gleaming white slope. Orange algae thrive in the heated water and give off color as vivid as the incandescence of a lava flow.

At dusk we make our way a mile or two farther on through the woods and come to a grassy swale where Witch Creek flows. Waters from heated springs upstream have warmed the creek to a temperature of 88°, and here at last we indulge in the luxury of bathing. But the light has almost gone, and we do not stay long. It is nearly dark by the time we return to the shore of the lake, refreshed, exhilarated, exhausted.

The wind dies down. Two giant moons appear, one over the trees and one in the water of the lake, the lower one a liquid, rippling moon that flows apart and comes together again at the will of the waves. Back in the woods, which are illuminated in a ghostly glow, there is a faint hiss of steam and a gentle splashing of waters. Rustic Geyser is erupting once again.

Good Tidings

August 18.   Sunrise over Heart Lake is moonset over Mount Sheridan: the pale orange moon drops slowly over the shoulder of the mountain, which is itself engulfed in a golden glow from the sun. Beneath all this, the broad green meadow by Witch Creek glows with streaks of yellow light while gray shadows of trees fall back from the rising sun.

The wind is calm as we set off on the last leg of the journey. And so are we. "Fear nothing," wrote the eminent naturalist and conservationist, John Muir, in his book *Our National Parks*. "No town park you have been accustomed to saunter in is so free from danger as the Yellowstone. It is a hard place to leave."

But leave we must, as every visitor must. Of the passing of our five parties of one, only footprints remain; the refuse that couldn't be burned is being packed out. For a memorable week we have watched the mountain ecosystem at work, seen the refreshing freedom of the wildlife, and for all that felt freer ourselves. We have reconfirmed the fact that nature does not exist exclusively for the pleasure of man.

Each of us carries away an inventory of meadows, mountains, forests, rivers, lakes, and geyser basins. By submerging into the ensemble of environments we came as close as possible to living more lives than one.

Here the views, the earth, the sky, are undisrupted, as the Wilderness Act of 1964 said they should be; this is an area where the earth and its community of life are untrammeled by man, where man himself is a visitor who does not remain, where the primeval character and solitude are retained.

As we come up out of Heart Lake Basin and head for home, Muir's famous quotation fits our mood exactly. "Climb the mountains and get their good tidings," he wrote in his description of Yellowstone National Park. "Nature's peace will flow into you as sunshine flows into trees. The winds will blow their own freshness into you, and the storms their energy, while cares will drop off like autumn leaves."

Boiling water from Rustic Geyser, near Heart Lake, bathes a fragile yet stable community of orange algae.

2

High Country

If there is a single lasting impression one gets from Yellowstone, it is a feeling of size. It is not that the park is in actual square miles all that large. After all, what is big to an American who can casually fly from New York to San Francisco in an afternoon? Rather, it is a feeling of bigness that comes from the park's almost infinite variety of topography and natural features, its unending richness of mountains, valleys, waterfalls, streams, forests, plateaus, lakes, canyons and springs.

It seemed incredible that we had penetrated less than one tenth of the Yellowstone wilderness. But it was true: we had traversed only the southeastern corner of the park. A week could have been spent in the southwestern corner, exploring the Bechler River region, and even that would have been too short a time. Or we would have liked a week of climbing in the Gallatin Range, or more time to explore the Lamar Valley and its tributaries, or to climb additional summits in the Absaroka Range.

Yellowstone National Park, roughly in the shape of a square, measures about sixty miles along each side, and within this territory our trip through the Thorofare country was only a beginning. But it was a fair introduction, for in the rest of the park are other valleys as wide and beautiful as that of the Upper Yellowstone and ridges whose summits are as commanding as that of Big Game Ridge. On the other hand, there were aspects of the park that we could not have seen in the Thorofare; for example, waterfalls. The Upper and Lower Falls of the Yellowstone River, 109 and 308 feet high respectively, are widely known, but the Bechler River region possesses thundering cascades in a remote wilderness setting. Iris and Colonnade falls are among the best of these. They seem to glide out of the forest onto a gray platform of lava and then plunge, like lesser Niagaras, into amphitheaters that collect the sound, amplify it, and project it as a booming roar. Both of these falls can be reached by trail, but dozens of others are accessible only by scrambling over wild terrain and climbing into canyons seldom visited by man. For-

Volcanic ridges and eroding plateaus constitute the basic topography of Yellowstone National Park. *Overleaf*: Cliffs, slopes, canyons—every topographic niche in Yellowstone is occupied by some form of wildlife.

Above: Blue lupine and red paintbrush rank among the most common summer flowers of Yellowstone. *Left*: At Colonnade Falls, the Bechler River plunges a hundred feet into a lava-ringed amphitheatre.

tunately for most visitors, one spectacular cascade in the Bechler region is accessible by paved road: Cave Falls, 300 feet across.

Most of these streams and waterfalls originate among the high volcanic plateaus, another major feature of Yellowstone. For the most part these are elongated, flat-topped ridges, clad with stands of lodgepole pine, as we had seen in crossing the Two Ocean Plateau near Mariposa Lake. For reasons not well understood, however, some lack dense forests; a good example of this is the Pitchstone Plateau, in the southern part of the park. On other plateaus, the lodgepole groves are broken by broad expanses of meadow or by the whitened crusts of thermal flats. In any case, the plateaus are about the only reasonably level terrain amid this high country, with the exception of a few broad valleys along the Yellowstone, Madison, and Lamar rivers.

The rest of Yellowstone National Park is mountainous—or under water. One tenth, more or less, is submerged beneath lakes and streams. Owing to heavy precipitation, mostly as snow on high peaks, several complex stream systems have become established, but the waters from them do not all reach the same destination. The Continental Divide, that "roof of the continent" that separates the collected mountain waters into Atlantic or Pacific drainages, passes diagonally through the park. North and east of it, all waters flow down the Madison and Yellowstone river systems, then down the Missouri and Mississippi to the Gulf of Mexico. Waters south and west of the Continental Divide flow into Snake River drainage and then down the Columbia River to the Pacific Ocean.

The most spectacular mountain peaks in the park are located along the eastern boundary, in the Absaroka Range. There are other high points, however, where a visitor can obtain commanding views of the Yellowstone landscape—such as from atop Mount Sheridan, which we passed on our Thorofare trip. A series of rugged peaks—the Gallatin Range—dominates the northwest corner of the park, and

these, like some of the others, are accessible by trail. We climbed to the summit of Avalanche Peak, in the heart of the Absaroka Range, and even though we were caught in an icy summer shower, we came away with lasting impressions of this wild territory.

The early Indians revered the high country of Yellowstone; they believed that from such elevations one could see into the next world. One can, at least, see into three states, and the views verify the salient feature of Yellowstone—its undisturbed immensity. Our favorite viewpoint is the summit of Mount Washburn. This isolated peak is high enough, 10,243 feet, and so centrally located that from the top of it we can see nearly all of the park. The mountain itself is accessible by easy trail and by park buses. Much preferable is to climb the peak on foot, although hikers unaccustomed to activity at high altitude should move with care.

Hiking slowly is the whole point anyway, lest we miss the life that abounds in the gentle spruce-fir forest that hugs the slopes up to 9,000 feet, or the tortured yet fascinating shapes of the rocks and vegetation above tree line. Here the weathering process—freezing, cracking, wedging, thawing—has split the rocks into sharp-edged slabs, and we must be careful of them as we climb. Ascending the mountain, we marvel at how the avens, a plant that pioneers where few others survive, secures a roothold and ultimately helps establish a thriving tundra ecosystem. The piping call of the pika, a diminutive mammal that abounds in high rocky places, has an almost echoing quality to it, as though one animal were answering another across the jagged slopes. These industrious relatives of the rabbit gather whatever forage the mountains produce and pile it away like Swiss mountaineers, to be utilized especially during the winter.

Finally, tired but exhilarated, we arrive at the summit. "The view is simply sublime," said General William Tecumseh Sherman, the Union commander of Civil War fame, when he came to the top in 1877, "worth the labor of reaching it *once*, but not *twice*.

I do not propose to try it again." If one can climb but one mountain in Yellowstone, it should be Mount Washburn. Looking out across the landscape gave us the feeling that we were riding a wave crest on a sea of trees. Lodgepoles cover the land toward every horizon, their dominance broken here and there by treeless summits thrust up out of the woods. Meadows show up clearly as bright green openings, irregular in outline. On one of them we can see with binoculars the prowlings of a grizzly as it searches for roots among the grasses.

Below us to the east, a great gash in the earth disrupts the continuity of the forest. It is the Grand Canyon of the Yellowstone River, but from here we see few of the bright colors so overwhelmingly visible at the rim of the canyon itself. At the northern end of the long expanse of the Mirror Plateau is Specimen Ridge, a name that puzzles us until we consult a map and note the names of streams that drain it: Crystal, Agate, Amethyst, Quartz, Flint, and Chalcedony creeks. Actually the ridge contains an astonishing series of petrified wood deposits, and we make a mental note to hike there as soon as possible.

Beyond the Mirror Plateau the horizon is a series of sharp-peaked remnants of the Absaroka Plateau, punctuated by glistening patches of snow in sheltered coves. Far to the south, almost obscured by bluish haze, is the Teton Range, and in front of that, the Red Mountains, of which Mount Sheridan, now far away, is the highest peak. A thousand sights and shapes and forms unfold if we stop for a while and use binoculars to bring the scenes below into sharper focus. There is the Hayden Valley, directly south, with wide pools of the Yellowstone River decorating it like shining mirrors. To the southwest runs the long and virtually uninterrupted surface of the Madison Plateau, and to the west rise the treeless peaks of the Gallatin Range.

Suddenly we detect a plume of white against the dark green forest. If we watch long enough, we see it expand and drift a trifle, then dissipate. It is a geyser, but which one? While we try to locate it with maps and arrows and compass, another tassel of steam comes out of the trees more directly to the west, and we conclude that something is erupting in the Norris Geyser Basin. We scan the horizon again and see other steam, though only wisps that represent small thermal areas.

Meanwhile, a movement nearby distracts us and we find a herd of bighorn passing not thirty steps away, seemingly oblivious of our presence, moving along the slope in search of fresh grass.

Thus, Yellowstone has more natural objects and values than we can readily see and enjoy. And since these features are preserved by law, the benefits of them are accruing to large numbers of people.

Coyote's Prophecy

"In generations to come, this place around here will be a treasure of the people. They will be proud of it and of all the curious things in it—flint rocks, hot springs, and cold springs."

So goes the old Indian legend, "Coyote's Prophecy Concerning Yellowstone Park." According to the story, Coyote came into this area, subdued Grizzly Bear, the incumbent chief of the inhabitants, and appointed Golden Eagle to assume command. "People will be proud of this spot," he went on. "Springs will bubble out, and steam will shoot out. Hot springs and cold springs will be side by side. Hot water will fly into the air, in this place and that place. No one knows how long this will continue. And voices will be heard here, in different languages, in the generations to come."

Today Coyote's prophecy has come true, and more than 2 million people visit Yellowstone National Park annually. For the most part, however, they limit their visits to the geyser basins and the Grand Canyon of the Yellowstone. Very few climb Mount Washburn, and fewer still go into the Thorofare country. For some visitors, Yellowstone is confusing or even frightening. A few explorers actually feared the geysers, thinking the steam toxic, and referred to the thermal basins as "death valleys." Others said that the scenery

Left: Morning mists sift through the marshes fringing Shoshone Lake, a haven for sandhill cranes and other waterfowl. *Above*: Ponds and wet meadows are favored by sandhill cranes, which breed and raise their young in Yellowstone during the summer.

would "cause anyone to shudder," that the mud volcanoes were "a most repulsive and terrifying sight," that the Grand Canyon of the Yellowstone River was a "fearful chasm."

There is little wonder that men have had mixed reactions to Yellowstone, for like most of the American West it is a place of enormous contrasts. It can be both savage and exquisitely beautiful, often at the same time. Unfortunately, most people do not see Yellowstone at the best time of year or the best time of day. They come in summer, for example, when the birds are quietly nesting back in the woods, and therefore they miss some of the music of mating time. Most of the large animals have migrated to the park's highlands, far from any road. And in July and August visitors miss the spring that has gone up the mountains earlier and the autumn that will come down later.

Yet each season brings its own special character to Yellowstone. By June the last of the migratory birds have arrived from the south—pelicans, ospreys, sandhill cranes, goldfinches, nighthawks, and a dozen kinds of flycatchers and warblers—and have started building their nests. Some resident nutcrackers, jays, owls, and geese may even have produced their young by this time.

As July arrives, there is an upward progress of paintbrush, wild geranium, sunflower, and other blooms. Although some species of flowers diminish at lower elevations, others burst forth on the mountain slopes. Calypso orchids, for example, become abundant at secluded locations in fir forests. July is the month of young birds, when robins and bluebirds leave their nests, and when gulls and pelicans rear their young on the Molly Islands in Yellowstone Lake.

In August, summer reaches its height on the high plateaus and mountain peaks. Wintergreen and kinnikinnick ripen. Young birds leave their nests. Adult birds moult. At the highest elevations, between 10,000 and 11,000 feet, no trees grow, but an abundance of vegetation thrives briefly. August also signals the beginning of autumn. In fact, the arrival of the first willet in July sometimes heralds the opening of fall migration, as shore birds and waders start to move south. Swallows depart in August, as do hummingbirds, sandpipers, tanagers, and some of the warblers.

With September, autumn color bursts out in the high places and rapidly works its way down the mountains. By this time nearly all young birds are out of their nests, with the exception perhaps of a few ospreys. Flights of migrating birds pass through, including flocks of juncos, Brewer's blackbirds, and white-crowned sparrows. Species such as elk that spent the summer at high elevations begin to come back down, while ducks and geese on their way south show up on ponds, lakes, and streams.

And then one day, in the soggy meadows beside the Bechler River, the last of the sandhill cranes will lift their great gray wings and climb up over the bordering lodgepole pines and soar off into the sky. Perhaps for one last time they will produce the resonant notes of their hooting, which all summer came across the meadows, one moment weakened and carried away, one moment amplified by the wind. And as the endless cycle of seasons turns to winter, Yellowstone will change again.

Coyote's prophecy has come true, and Yellowstone has become a treasure of the people, perhaps as much for its immensity as for its thermal wonders, its wildlife, and its peace and quiet. Yet the peace is something of a paradox, for Yellowstone has not always been a quiet land; it was once the site of some of the greatest violence the world has ever known.

From the summit of Mount Washburn the Grand Canyon of the Yellowstone River appears as a great gash through the volcanic plateau.

3

Fire and Brimstone

Perhaps nowhere else in the Rocky Mountains have the volcanic forces been so busy.

JOHN MUIR, *Our National Parks*, 1901

The peace and solitude are deceptive. These quiet ridges and level terraces were thrown out—or up—in one of the most violent eras of volcanism known to the science of geology. So gigantic were the upheavals and blasts that devastated this high country that the average human being, unless he has been exposed to the "exploding worlds" of science fiction, can only grope for comprehension. Nothing like it has ever been recorded by man. Moreover, clear-cut records in the rocks, still available for all to see, indicate that this violence occurred, on and off, for more than a million years.

Today some of the evidence is covered up or eroded away, but the remaining signs are unmistakable. Below Mount Washburn, for example, is the edge of an elliptical volcanic crater that is very close to being the largest in the world. Although we can hardly follow the rim of it, professional geologists have mapped this area in detail and through meticulous reconstruction can trace nearly its entire periphery, measuring it on the long diameter at fifty miles, and on the shorter axis at thirty. Moreover, this huge crater, or, more appropriately, caldera, was formed during the last of three volcanic cycles, the first of which took place about 2 million years ago. All were catastrophic outbursts of tremendous volume, and none took more than a day or a week, apparently, to happen. Each ejected enormous masses of volcanic debris, after which the "roof" rocks that had once lain over those masses collapsed. The result was a great bowl-shaped caldera.

It is difficult to compare these prehistoric eruptions with modern ones. The greatest explosion of historic times was probably that of Krakatoa, a volcanic island in the Sunda Straits of Java, which erupted in 1883. The roar was heard in Australia, three thousand miles away. Dust and ash clouds, rising to as much as fifty miles in altitude, went windborne around the globe. After large amounts of pumice and volcanic ash from deep within the earth were thrown out, much of the rock of the island itself, including eight square miles of land, apparently sank into the

The Grand Canyon of the Yellowstone River exposes baked and disintegrating rhyolite lava.

Above: Where volcanic
eruptions once hurled lava
skyward, golden-mantled
ground squirrels and other
animals now peacefully
occupy forest glades and rocky
slopes. *Right*: Tower Creek
has cut its way through layers
of broken lava fragments.

hole thus formed. Yet those upheavals, immense as they were, seem puny compared with those that once shook the Rocky Mountains. Geologists believe that the Yellowstone eruptions were about 200 times as large as those of Krakatoa.

The Great Volcanic Eruptions

Little is known about the sources of the first eruptions, 2 million years ago, but something on the order of several hundred cubic miles of pumice and ash were ejected in a very short time, probably from within the present park, but extending west to the Island Park area. The second cycle of explosive volcanism, about 1.2 million years ago, was centered in the Island Park area, just outside Yellowstone National Park. The rim of this crater is also partly buried by younger rocks, but through anomalies in the earth's gravity field its buried portions can be inferred.

The third cycle of explosive eruptions and roof rock collapses, which occurred about 600,000 years ago as dated by radiometric measurements of the rocks, accounts for much of Yellowstone as it is today. Like the others, it probably began with an upsurge of magma, or molten rock, to form large subterranean reservoirs. In all likelihood, such insurgence would have been visible on the surface of the earth as a dome-like mountain fifty to seventy miles across. This action of doming must have subjected the surface rocks to more of a strain than they could take. They fractured, or faulted, in a ring around the apex of the dome, reducing the ability of the surface structure to contain the powerfully surging lava beneath. There were some initial flows of rhyolite, a rock of the same composition as granite, but these were only leaks that reached the surface.

Finally, the great eruption may have begun as Krakatoa began: rumbling, smoking, ejection of tons of debris that darkened the sky, lightning, thunder. Not long after that came the main explosions—fragments of ash, crystals, and pumice hurled out in a blinding flare of exploding gas. This gas erupted not only around the fragmental debris but also within it,

due to expanding pockets of volatile material. This mixture of gas, solid particles, and superheated steam flew out over the land, devastating every living thing for miles around. Dust and smoke doubtless darkened the skies; ash fell and formed sizable deposits as far away as what are now Kansas and Nebraska.

This great ash flow was propelled down slopes and valleys and around mountains at speeds that may have exceeded a hundred miles an hour. The best-known historic parallel to this kind of glowing, exploding-cloud eruption, though miniature by comparison, is the eruption in 1902 of Mont Pelée, on the Caribbean island of Martinique. Of that event an eyewitness said: "A considerable cloud . . . developed almost as rapidly in height as in length. Innumerable electric scintillations played through the chaos of vapors, at the same time that the ears were deafened by a frightful fracas." The incandescent cloud of gas and ash from Mont Pelée destroyed all but two of the thirty thousand inhabitants in the city of Saint Pierre, five miles away. Had there been any human beings as near to Yellowstone when its eruption occurred, they too would have been incinerated on the spot.

The mass of ash and pumice and gas eventually came to a halt, cooled off a trifle, became glassy and sticky, collapsed under its own weight, and literally welded itself together into a rock called welded tuff. After the molten material—many cubic miles of it—was disgorged, the dome that had swelled up over the surging magma collapsed to form the giant caldera. This smoking pit must have measured fifty miles across and about a mile deep. The only caldera known to exceed this size is one sixty miles in diameter, occupied by Lake Toba, in Sumatra.

Almost immediately the collapse of the caldera triggered another series of eruptions. New ash flows burst from the cracks and vents and welded themselves to the earlier flows that had not had time to cool and solidify. This material extends around the walls of the caldera and permits a fairly accurate identification of the size and extent of the crater, its collapse, and its flows.

Lava Flows and Glass Mountains

After the massive expulsion of ash-flow tuff and the falling in of the caldera, there followed a long period of volcanism in which lavas were erupted through the same fractures into the caldera. Yet the old gas pressures were gone and the new outpourings were not as lively—mostly quiet flows of sticky, viscous, slow-moving rhyolite. Some of them, though nonviolent, were nevertheless enormous—up to thirty miles across.

This rhyolite, which constitutes so much of Yellowstone's surface, is a combination of quartz and feldspar, chemically the same as granite but forming only after magma has burst out on the surface of the earth. Sometimes, in less violent eruptions, rhyolite has a taffy-like consistency and piles up in a heap or flows out in tongues of lava that are deeply lobed and steep at the front. Persistent squeezing pushes up ridges; on the Pitchstone Plateau, pressure ridges were elevated in concentric patterns around the vent from which the lava came.

Some rhyolite emerged in nearly liquid form, which cooled and hardened rapidly into a black or brown glass called obsidian. But rhyolite is variable; in places it is coarse enough to resemble concrete. A conglomeration of jumbled, cemented fragments, as seen in the Firehole Canyon, resulted when the moving flow crusted over, broke, and carried with it broken pieces of crust. Deposits of this material are known as rhyolite breccia.

The Yellowstone lavas have long since cooled and solidified, but a perceptive visitor today cannot help but be fascinated by their variation and beauty. A good place to study them is on the way into Shoshone Geyser Basin. The flow structure, arrangement of minerals, and weathered forms are all there, beneath or beside a hiker's feet, all attesting to that moment when the lava stopped—more than 100,000 years ago in this part of the park. Quite often the rhyolite contains chunks of black obsidian, which look like marbles mixed in fudge. There is so much of this that the Shoshone trail turns black in places, and the hiker literally walks on glass. If he kneels and looks more closely, he is apt to discern lovely, intricate structural designs in the lava that are seldom or never the same: arches, loops, waves, dips, bands, and curls. In places the designs might remind him of graphic granite in the hills of New England.

Of such materials was the last caldera formed. Its thirty-by-fifty-mile rim may be followed roughly along the Madison Canyon past Mount Haynes, up through the Norris area, north of the Grand Canyon of the Yellowstone, past the front of Mount Washburn, east of Broad Creek, through the Yellowstone Lake area from Lake Butte to Flat Mountain, then down past the Red Mountains. Yet the caldera is not readily detected today because later lava flows filled it up and in places overflowed the rim, which is why we do not see the southwestern margin.

Today Yellowstone is at the end of a volcanic cycle: the heated ground, the thermal areas, the hot springs and geysers, are evidence that magma is still present at depth. Some say that Yellowstone represents a waning, dying stage of action. But since the cycle has repeated itself in history, we may well wonder if it will stop dying and begin heating up again. The answer to that is not known, but change is going on, and perhaps man's lifetime, or even generations of lifetimes, are too short to detect a significant trend. How many past Old Faithfuls there have been is anybody's guess—perhaps thousands.

Cracks in the Earth

Reflecting on these great convulsions, we may ask why the eruptions were so devastating in this particular area. Most volcanic eruptions are closer to the sea, or to areas of more active mountain-building, such as around the Pacific Ocean basin. As it happens, Yellowstone's volcanoes are extremely young, geologically speaking; 2 million years, the age of the first explosive eruption, is nothing compared with the age of other volcanoes in this area, or with the age of the earth itself. And since the region is so young, it is still cracking, splitting, upheaving, and shaking, in the process that makes mountains.

Top: Lichens mantle nearly every exposed rock surface, adding to Yellowstone's treasury of form and design. *Bottom*: At Obsidian Cliff, flows of rhyolite and volcanic glass have congealed in twisted patterns. *Right*: Sheepeater Cliffs are the edge of a basaltic lava flow that cooled into columns.

That rare phenomenon—standing petrified trees—is not so rare at Yellowstone. *Right*: Twenty-seven forests were buried and fossilized in one locality, and are being uncovered by erosion. *Above*: In cross-section a petrified tree stump reveals the finely preserved structural details of the ancient wood.

Geologists infer that there is a creeping split in the earth's crust in this region, a slow and gradual pulling apart along a line that extends from southwest of the park to its northeastern corner. Not only has this series of faults opened toward the northeast, but it has intersected other geological structures from the northwest. At such intersections, conditions are highly favorable for the upwelling of magma bodies, and since Yellowstone has already been cracked in circular patterns, we can well expect some of the materials inside the earth to emerge. The crustal splitting appears to have started in southern Idaho 10 to 15 million years ago and has extended northeastward ever since. On reaching the other fault line, a zone represented in a more modern time by the Hebgen Lake earthquake of 1959, the supervolcanic events took place.

None of these cycles tells us when the Yellowstone region may have another climactic, ash-flow type of eruption. But geologists are inclined to think that another big blast is not very imminent. It is reasonable to assume that Yellowstone is in for more volcanic activity, but perhaps the greater likelihood is for marginal volcanism such as small basalt flows and nonviolent rhyolite outpourings.

With scientific equipment now measuring daily movements of the earth in Yellowstone National Park, man is not apt to be caught by surprise. As research funds permit, geologists hope to determine the exact locations and sizes of the remaining magma bodies. This is normally done by determining how acoustical waves generated by a small man-made explosion travel through the earth. Such waves move differently through liquid, molten rock than through rock that has been solidified. By analyzing the differences it may be possible to infer not only the whereabouts but the depth of the magma as well. It is presently assumed that the main magmatic body lies beneath the central part of Yellowstone at a depth of several thousand feet. If more lava flows, it will in all likelihood be rhyolite. But we should not get the impression that Yellowstone is solely a rhyolite-

Quiet, a gentle mist, a warm sun: three reasons for hiking along
the canyon rim at sunrise.

covered region, or even that it is entirely volcanic. Although most spectacular in origin, and capturing our attention first, the volcanic rocks are of relatively recent times. Rocks of nearly every age occur in Yellowstone.

The oldest rocks in the park are gneiss, a form of metamorphosed granite, which may be seen in the canyon of the Lamar River along the northeast entrance highway. Its age is approximately 2.7 billion years. From that time up to the present, the geologic history of the region has been one of repeated sinkings into the ocean. The Laramide Revolution, or orogeny, a period of extensive mountain building that began about 75 million years ago and lasted 20 million years, pushed up such ranges as the neighboring Big Horn, Beartooth, and Wind River mountains. And there was volcanism long before the big ash blowouts; the eruptions in the Absaroka Mountains 40 to 50 million years ago came not primarily as clouds of exploding ash and gas but as wide outpourings of lavas and volcanic mudflows, like the Cascade Range today. Cone-shaped volcanoes, not unlike Mount Hood, Mount Rainier, or Fujiyama, poured out enormous masses of andesite and basalt rather than rhyolite. One after another, Absaroka volcanoes gave up their molten matter and built a vast plateau of breccias, cinders, and lava flows to a thickness of several thousand feet, covering all of Yellowstone.

Petrified Forests

Although not always violent, these volcanoes frequently sent out clouds of dust and ash that blanketed the neighboring landscape, trees and all. Specimen Ridge, in the north central part of the park, is very well named, because specimens galore of trees, now petrified, may be found here. A number of fossil forests occur in Yellowstone National Park; their aggregate area is in excess of forty square miles—the largest known fossil forest. What makes them unusual and valuable is that many of the trees still stand. The Petrified Forest of Arizona is a collection of fallen logs; the trees once standing at Florissant Fossil Beds in Colorado have been torn down by vandals. Yellowstone National Park has enjoyed substantial protection for more than a century, and so it is possible to hike up the ridges, meadows, and sagebrush slopes to see the stumps where they grew many millions of years ago. It is an impressive experience, but even more astounding is the discovery that not just one forest was blanketed with cinders here; there are twenty-seven, one on top of another, layer by layer, to a thickness of 1,200 feet.

This suggests that after each eruption and the subsequent fall of debris there was an interim of quiet during which the forests grew anew, burgeoning in the fresh volcanic soil. Perhaps a number of forests lived for centuries or millenniums before the skies grew dark again with suffocating dust. Time and again it happened, the only place in the world, say geologists, where there are so many petrified forests exposed, one on top of another, in original positions of growth.

The result of sudden suffocation is a landscape halted in place and time; the scene was buried, not destroyed, just as showers of ash from Vesuvius so thoroughly and delicately preserved Pompeii. In Yellowstone, fossilized leaves, twigs, needles, cones, and seeds have been found, representing more than a hundred species of trees and shrubs: redwoods, sycamores, walnuts, magnolias, chestnuts, and oaks—species typical of warm, wet forests today. Thus in the dust of Yellowstone lie the visible remains of a gentle world where redwoods grew to be five feet or more in diameter and at least a thousand years old.

All of this Absaroka volcanism took place over millions of years, during which there must have been long pauses with few or no eruptions. But action of another type went on, for everything that comes to the surface of this planet is attacked by the scouring, rearranging forces of erosion. Old volcanic deposits that once lay over the Yellowstone area were stripped away by streams, which doubtless carried away the remains of additional forests. Much of the wood was silicified by steady seepage over the centuries, turning

into stone so slowly that the structure of the wood has been preserved. But water was also wearing away the whole plateau, and in time the glaciers of the Ice Age would have their effect. The Absarokas ultimately took on an aspect of sharp-peaked, glaciated mountains, losing their original gentle profile of a volcanic plateau.

Grand Canyon of the Yellowstone

All this early regional volcanism was only a prelude to the violent explosions of which we have already spoken, which helped build up the modern landscape in the park itself. After the recent super-eruptions died away 600,000 years ago, and the ash-flow tuffs had cooled and hardened, there was a time of quiet. But then magma surged up again, though not as forcefully as before, and during subsequent years approximately thirty different flows took place, each with its own specific center of eruption. The last occurred about 75,000 years ago. These issued mostly from the ring fractures of the huge caldera, flowing quietly but relentlessly and spreading out on the sunken floor of the ancient crater.

A lake formed there also. Water accumulated within the caldera, filled it, and finally poured over the crater rim through the lowest available spillway. As time went on, the Yellowstone River cut headward from the north, tapping the lake and lowering it as the river opened a sizeable canyon that grew to be about fifteen miles in length. This is the Grand Canyon of the Yellowstone River.

The familiar yellow-colored section of this canyon, as seen from Artist Point or Inspiration Point, lies over one of the ring fracture zones, which in turn lies above the magma masses. Hot water has for millenniums welled up into these rocks, boiling and baking them, changing the constituents physically as well as chemically, a process known as hydrothermal alteration. The brown and gray rock of the original rhyolite flow turned to a brilliant yellow stone, from which the region got its name. There are other colors as well—grays, oranges, and pinks—but the predominant hue is yellow. The rock thus weakened has been partly carried away by the erosive power of the river, which has a gradient of as much as eighty feet per mile.

The rhyolite at the head of the canyon has not been so altered and weakened, and so it erodes more slowly than the baked yellow stone below. That leaves a lip, or stairstep, of harder, denser rock over which the Yellowstone River flows—which accounts for the Lower Falls. The Upper Falls, a half mile away, have almost the same origin, except that the difference in hardness of rock comes from a difference in crystal structure between two parts of a rhyolite flow.

The Glaciers: Ice and Steam

Both of these waterfalls and the canyon itself were overwhelmed when glaciers invaded the region in three major cycles during the period between 12,000 and 350,000 years ago. Ice came from sources to the north and south, and as temperatures decreased, accumulations of snow and ice increased. The uplands collected and retained more snow in winter than melted throughout the summer, and the Yellowstone region was soon weighted down with sheets of ice as thick as three thousand feet.

Lobes from glaciers and caps of ice moved downstream drainages such as the Madison River. Under the plucking, scouring, scraping action of the glacier, Madison River Canyon became a U-shaped valley, typical of glaciated landscapes. As luck would have it, ice flowed into the Grand Canyon of the Yellowstone River but never turned and flowed downstream. If it had, the V-shaped gorge we know today would have been scooped out into a U-shaped valley like that of the Madison River.

During each glaciation, Yellowstone was almost completely covered by ice, and even Mount Washburn was engulfed. Ice flowed from caps on the highest peaks and plateaus and accumulated to enormous depths in the basin of Yellowstone Lake. As climates warmed, the glaciers stagnated, melted, and receded, leaving the lava landscape altered but not destroyed. There is in places glacial sculpture as well as scratches

made by rocks held tightly in the moving ice. Here, as in few places in the world, lava occasionally poured out against the ice, a phenomenon that allows some excellent correlations between times of ice flow and times of lava flow. Such comparisons support rather precise dating of events, thanks to sophisticated techniques that measure radioisotopes and their decay products in rocks.

The glaciers, in addition to scraping away certain portions of the topography, also added to the landscape. The ice transported large boulders long distances and when it melted released them helter-skelter in the valleys and along the plateaus. These are glacial erratics—erratic in the sense that they were brought by the ice from a distant source, far from the place where they now occur. The largest erratics ultimately came to have a beneficent role in the biological history of the Lamar Valley, for they sheltered the seedlings of trees so well that today one gets the impression that each erratic has a Douglas fir growing beside it.

And so ends, more or less, Yellowstone's volcanic history. Now the ice has gone, but the heat has not. The magma, somewhere below, still remains far closer to the surface than in most other regions on earth. There is no evidence that the ground is cooling or that the old volcanoes are dead. Yellowstone may be only in an interphase. Some parts appear to be heating up again while others cool off. Earthquakes still occur. We can only speculate; after all, man has been in this region for only a few thousand years at most and has studied it systematically only during the past century. Such short observation makes recognition of long-range trends in the regimen of the earth very difficult. Until additional information is available, we can say only that more fire and brimstone will be produced someday.

In the meanwhile, water falling on the surface of this high country percolates into the lava flows and meets the heat of the magma below. The result of that encounter is a change of scene from the smoking landscape of yesteryear to the steaming one of today.

4

Roaring Basins

For ten successive times this gorgeous display was repeated. At the end of this time, I found myself quite weak from excitement.

WILLIAM HENRY HOLMES,
diary, 1878

Any mountainous area at this latitude (45°, halfway to the North Pole) and altitude (6,000 to 13,000 feet) is bound to receive a considerable amount of moisture each year, much of it snow. The heaviest seasonal snowfall on record in Yellowstone National Park was more than twenty-two feet at the Lake Ranger Station in 1909, but the United States Weather Bureau reported that local areas higher in the mountains receive more than thirty feet annually. Snow has fallen, somewhere in the park, during every month of the year, and raging blizzards can be experienced in June and September. The annual precipitation for high country, such as that around Old Faithful, in the Upper Geyser Basin, is eighteen to twenty inches.

All this precipitation yields a tremendous run-off, which is usually measured in terms of an acre foot—the volume of water required to cover an area of one acre to a depth of one foot. The Yellowstone River has a flow of more than 2 million acre feet per year, the Snake River nearly 1 million, the Falls River 500,000, and the Madison almost 400,000, where they leave the park. This means that the major streams alone carry away nearly 4 million acre feet of water a year.

These rivers are fed by springs, as most rivers are, and there would be little unusual about all the wetness and run-off except for the legacy of the era of volcanism: underground heat. All parts of the earth radiate some warmth, but scientific measurements have shown that the amount of heat given off by the Upper Geyser Basin is about fifty times that given off by regions where there are no thermal features. Moreover, geological evidence suggests that this area has been exceedingly hot for 2 million years or more.

The falling waters and melting snows that do not run off immediately in streams sink down through the porous volcanic rock and descend until they reach the water table, a level beneath which the rocks are saturated. There the water slows its movement, but that is not the end of the journey. Ground water itself circulates. It goes wherever it can, up, down, forward, backward, or sideways, its restless currents impelled

Old Faithful Geyser at sunset.

by variations in pressure and temperature. Some pours out of the ground as cold springs, swelling the tributaries of major rivers. Some gets caught, perhaps in underground pockets, and remains there a long time. Indeed, some of the waters issuing from Yellowstone's basins may have been underground for hundreds of years.

How Geysers Erupt

Inevitably, a great deal·of this water goes deeper and deeper—perhaps to 10,000 feet—and gets hotter and hotter as it contacts the heated rocks below. In fact, it gets so hot and is under such pressure from the water above that it passes the sea level boiling temperature of 212° F. and may go higher than 500° F. But at great depths it cannot boil; it cannot turn to steam since the pressure is too confining. Nevertheless, this water has a place to go, and that is one of the secrets of Yellowstone. Thanks to convection currents and to openings at the surface, this superheated water comes back up and out of the ground. As it rises through what is probably a complex subterranean system of conduits, pressure on it is reduced. With that, the water begins to boil violently. Balls of steam explode up out of the throats of a number of pools but vanish rapidly, and a trifle uncannily, before reaching the surface, for the relatively cooler water near the top causes the steam to condense to water. In other cases, steam does reach the surface, whereupon the water boils vigorously. Many pools are violently agitated, erupting and flinging out spray. In extraordinary instances, violent boiling churns the spring to great depths. If so much steam is formed that it cannot all bubble up *through* the water, it acts as a plunger, driving the water above it up and out of the spring as a geyser eruption.

That sounds very simple, but the actual process turns out to be more complex than men have dreamed —or measured. For example, the heat of the water at moderate, but not great, depths has been measured by United States Geological Survey researchers, who drilled test holes in the Norris Geyser Basin. They

recorded 465° F. at a depth of 1,088 feet, the lowest point they could reach, and the temperature had still been going up as the instruments went down.

Water at this temperature is lighter in weight than cool water. Hence, given an opening somewhere on the surface, it will rise and flow gently out in hot springs or catapult itself high into the air. Which of these it does depends on the configuration of the tube or tubes through which it must pass, and on the temperature, pressure, and content of steam. Pressure lessens as the water ascends, and the closer it gets to the surface, the lower is the temperature required to bring it to a boil. Released from confinement, some of the water may turn into steam, perhaps violently.

All this is a delicate operation. Should the superheated water cool off too much on the way up, there may not be sufficient steam to push it out of its vent, and so it oozes forth as a simple hot spring. But with enough steam energy left, a column of water can be expelled as a gushing fountain.

By this theory it can be inferred that if adequate heat energy is transferred to the water at depth and the conduits are relatively narrow, the steam will push up a substantial column of boiling water in an eruption that could last for quite some time. One of the best-known examples of this is Castle Geyser, which plays for sixty to eighty minutes. If the conduit is larger, greater amounts of steam may build up and blow out enormous volumes of water, which would then be like Giant Geyser, where a million gallons of water may be ejected over a period of about one and a half hours.

The point is that quite often a precarious balance exists between pressure and temperature, and that the system may blow at even the slightest change in this balance. When incoming waters fill the underground conduit system of a spring, all that may be needed is a pre-eruptive splash or two to reduce the pressure and upset the balance. Thereupon, a full-scale eruption occurs. As the channels are emptied and the energy spent, the geyser subsides, but there may still be pockets of very hot water that give off steam for a

Splashing hot water, with ample time between eruptions to evaporate
and deposit silica, has built an elaborate cone at Grotto Geyser.

long time following the initial eruption.

The mechanism that foments a geyser (a word that comes from the Icelandic *geysa*, "to gush") is probably contained within the upper two hundred feet of the surface of the earth, and this in turn draws water up from much greater depths. There is so much room for variation in the nature of the tubes, conduits, and channels, and in the amount, temperature, and pressure of water available that geyser actions vary considerably. Some are small and gentle, some regular, some irregular, some so violent that they rip loose portions of the vent, scattering fragments of rock in all directions and killing surrounding trees.

Predicting Geyser Eruptions

Some eruptions can be rather well predicted, even by the average person, if he observes how much water is expelled each time and how long a geyser takes to recharge its system. For example, if a geyser throws out an uncommonly large amount of water, we can assume that it has thoroughly drained itself and that an unusually long time will be required for water to accumulate again. If only a small amount of water is discharged, the time until the next eruption will be shorter. With a little practice on a short-cycle geyser, such as Minute Man in Shoshone Geyser Basin, the observer can predict eruptions seconds before they

Roaring Mountain roars much less each year as thermal energy
beneath it subsides.

occur. If he also keeps his eye on the amount of water in the "well," or throat, of the vent, he can usually be even more accurate, because some geysers well up gradually and overflow before erupting. There are other signals, too, in this complex process, and the experienced observer becomes familiar with all characteristics of the geyser he is watching before he predicts with any degree of certainty when it will go off again. That is why park naturalists often specify a period of an hour or so during which a specific geyser may erupt. Often one cannot be more precise.

With Old Faithful it is a little easier. Although this famous geyser does not erupt every hour on the hour, one can predict when it will erupt again—give or take five minutes—if he knows (1) the length of the previous interval, (2) the time the last eruption began, and (3) the duration of the eruption. Old Faithful's eruptions are short—only one and a half to five minutes in duration. But the column of boiling water is a magnificent sight, rising to at least 100 feet and sometimes almost 200. That height is somewhat dependent upon the wind, which can carry away the uppermost spray. The accompanying steam clouds climb much higher, and in winter the billows of vapor in icy air are even more voluminous.

The water that bursts from Old Faithful is hotter than boiling and varies in quantity from 10,000 to 12,000 gallons per eruption. This falls around the base of the geyser and shortly finds its way into the Firehole River.

The time schedule for this massive discharge is not as steady as the name of the geyser would suggest. In fact, there are other geysers in Yellowstone National Park that are more faithful than Old Faithful, with intervals between eruptions more nearly equal. The length of time between eruptions of Old Faithful may be from thirty-three to ninety-six minutes, more than an hour's possible variation. This, like other behavioral figures on this geyser's activities, is based on data from thousands of eruptions. From such observations we may assume that Old Faithful has erupted more than 800,000 times in the last century.

Obviously it has its own timetable of eruptions, and man's reading of this schedule is still imperfect. There are persons who visit Yellowstone periodically and vow that the geyser is no longer leaping as high as it used to, or that it misses an eruption now and then, and that therefore it is slowly dying—none of which is true. Geologists who have watched this geyser for decades, and have studied records that go back intermittently to the discovery of the Upper Geyser Basin, find no evidence that the amount of water per eruption is any less than it was or that Old Faithful has ever missed an eruption. As far as is known, it is as active now as when discovered. It is estimated to have been in existence for the past 200 to 300 years, despite the many earthquakes that have occurred in this region and might have altered it. The latest earthquake, in 1959, which centered in Hebgen Lake, Montana, thirty miles away, affected many of the springs in this area, but the only noticeable permanent effect on Old Faithful was to lengthen the geyser's average interval between eruptions from sixty to sixty-five minutes.

Old Faithful could quit at any time, of course. Any geyser could, and some have. Others have been born in recent years. Nature changes the underground channels and water flow without consulting men. Chances are, however, that Old Faithful will go on being faithful—more or less—for years to come.

Mysteries of Geysers

There are more than 200 geysers in Yellowstone National Park—a number greater than in any other region of the world—and they come in such assorted shapes and sizes that even if Old Faithful were to cease tomorrow, there would be some consolation in the fact that so many others remain. Some, indeed, are far more powerful and explosive than Old Faithful, and many erupt to greater heights. Giant Geyser, about a mile from Old Faithful, has erupted irregularly over the years, reaching as high as 250 feet. Even this is not the world's largest geyser. The mud lake eruptions in the crater of Poás Volcano, a national park in Costa Rica, may be larger; at least they seem to be when viewed from the crater rim half a mile away. The whole inner crater, nearly a quarter of a mile in diameter, is filled with flying mud and clouds of steam when a good-sized eruption occurs.

Excelsior Geyser in Yellowstone used to erupt perhaps as high as 300 feet but today is subdued, perhaps in a cycle of lesser activity. From its large and colorful crater boiling water flows at the rate of 4,000 gallons a minute, a far larger discharge than any other spring in the park.

Perhaps the most mysterious geyser in Yellowstone is the highest, Steamboat Geyser, whose eruptions have been known to reach 300 feet. Park people do not miss an eruption of this giant because the violence endures for hours and the roar can be heard for miles. Following each eruption is a powerful steam phase that lasts from several hours to more than a day. One question that cannot be answered is when Steamboat will erupt again. Prior to 1911 there were only five known eruptions, and between then and 1960 there were none. One eruption occurred in 1961 and that evidently ushered in a period of action, for from 1962 on, Steamboat erupted each year as follows: six times, then seventeen, twenty-nine, twenty-two, eleven, four, three, two. In 1970 the geyser was back down to zero again. Whether this means that Steamboat enters an active stage every fifty years or so only time will tell.

The largest eruption of all time was apparently Waimangu Geyser in New Zealand, which blew up to a height of more than 1,000 feet in 1909. Giantism or eccentricity is not, of course, the only criterion by which a geyser is judged. All have their fascinating features, and all are different. Grotto Geyser looks as though it is erupting from a weirdly shaped medieval castle, complete with moats and drawbridges. Riverside Geyser flings its waters out at an angle over the Firehole River. The vent of Atomizer Geyser is so small that water is ejected more like a spray than a fountain. Some geysers, such as Fan and Mortar, erupt simultaneously; others start a chain of eruptions from nearby vents. During a single eruption,

Castle Geyser in steam phase. *Overleaf*: At Mammoth Hot Springs, waters laden with calcium carbonate have deposited travertine terraces that are among the largest in the world.

certain geysers have explosive bursts, as many as three hundred. Sawmill Geyser jettisons its water in a circular motion from a funnel-shaped bowl.

Since geyser water is loaded with silica (silicon dioxide), the substance of which ordinary quartz sand is composed, one might assume that giant cones of siliceous sinter would be built up around the vent of every geyser. Yet some gigantic geysers erupt from pools that have no cones at all. Eruptions of great violence, perhaps earthquake inspired, may blow existing cones to bits, as happened with Sapphire Pool after the 1959 earthquake; hundreds of tons of sinter were ripped up and washed into the Firehole River. Apparently what it takes to build a giant cone, such as that around Lone Star Geyser, is an extended interval between eruptions, sufficient for the fallen water to evaporate and deposit its silica content, and time enough for many deposits to be laid down without disturbance. Persistent splashing, as in Castle Geyser, may also provide conditions for the growth of a cone.

With some geysers, such as Steamboat, it is difficult to discern a pattern in the intervals between eruptions or in the cycles between eruptive activity. For all its variations in eruption, Old Faithful is classed as a regular geyser, but Beehive is one of many whose eruptions are highly irregular. The early explorers considered Beehive one of the most spectacular and it surely remains so today. The smallness of its aperture accounts for release of water under a very high pressure with loud roaring. But Beehive has unpredictably gone through periods of activity and periods of dormancy. Man has been measuring the Yellowstone geysers for only a hundred years or so, and since the activity of some of them may be in cycles of centuries, there is still a great deal to be learned. By contrast, other geysers are constantly in eruption, among them Perpetual, Clepsydra, Bijou, and Little Whirligig. Occasionally a major geyser will go into an eruptive phase of long duration, as when the Giantess once erupted for more than a hundred hours.

Obviously one could spend a lifetime studying gey-sers. Dr. George Marler has done just about that in Yellowstone and has gained an extraordinary insight into the mechanics of thermal features. But even after more than thirty-five years of experience he is among the first to admit that man has much to learn. The visitor with limited time gets only an introduction to the most obvious features; even extending his stay for weeks would not do justice to all the geysers. Nevertheless, it is a unique experience to wander along the walks in these thermal basins. We once stayed to watch an eruption of Castle Geyser, and while it was playing, Old Faithful, Giantess, Plume, and Sawmill went into eruption almost simultaneously.

To us, some of the most interesting geysers are those that few people know about. They may be off in some remote place like the Shoshone Geyser Basin, accessible only by foot or canoe. They may have no names; some may be so small or so new or so inconspicuous as to command little attention. Yet we have stood beside them, watched the waters well up, heard the deep-throated guttural sounds as eruption roiled the surface, and then observed but the tiniest of fountains, perhaps no more than a foot in height. Yet somehow there is as much a miracle in these miniature geysers as in the large ones. Delicate silica lacework forms a fringe around many. The noises of water tumbling into and out of pools vary from spring to spring. Spray is hurled out differently every time, and we watch with great curiosity to see whether the next eruption will be any higher, wider, or louder than the previous one. Such curiosity can keep an observer occupied for hours.

The Thermal Springs

No one knows exactly how many thermal features there are in Yellowstone National Park, because they change, occur in hidden places, and vary from tiny heated seeps to highly explosive geysers. The best estimate, counting geysers, boiling pools, cauldrons, mud pots, sulfur pools, cinder pools, steam vents, and travertine springs, is that there are about 3,000 thermal features in the park.

Scalded trees succumb to the advance of thermal activity at New Highland Terrace, Mammoth Hot Springs.

Hot pools and paint pots get their colors from different sources: suspended particles, iron and sulfur compounds, algae, bacteria, and the scattered rays of sunlight reflecting from great depth. *Top and opposite*: Opalescent pools in Norris Geyser Basin. *Middle*: Evening Primrose Spring in Gibbon Geyser Basin. *Bottom*: Pool at Artist Paint Pots. *Overleaf*: Waters from Grand Prismatic Spring overflow onto the surrounding terrace where colorful beds of algae flourish.

Most of these are merely hot springs that do not erupt or exhibit more than a vigorous boiling. The most famous is Morning Glory Pool. Even though not the largest, deepest, or most colorful, it is one of the most accessible; and the blue and yellow colors within it are recalled long after a visit to Yellowstone has ended.

A little hiking and exploration will reveal a vast collection of pools in many combinations of colors. Explorers gave the names of precious stones to these pools—Emerald, Sapphire, Opal, Onyx, Beryl, Turquoise, Topaz, Pearl, Diamond—or names descriptive in other ways, such as Beauty, Chromatic, Brilliant, Rainbow.

Each pool has its special color. Some are nearly colorless, but they are rare; the rest range from a light touch of blue to deep blue to aquamarine to blue green and deep green, and there are red pools, yellow pools, brown pools, gray pools. Most of the color seems to be prismatic, refracted and reflected as light rays pass through the water or are bounced back from it. Where the walls of a spring have color, this affects the hue, and where the temperature of the water is such that algae can grow, they impart oranges, yellows, russet browns, or forest greens to the pools.

In some cases, particles in colloidal suspension produce a pool that appears milky and may have shades of blue, green, or brown. Minerals occur in the deposits around some springs, and indeed may be present in the pools, but they are not the major cause of color except in the sulfur and iron oxide pools.

Largest and most colorful of Yellowstone's thermal pools is Grand Prismatic Spring, 370 feet in diameter. It rests in the top of a wide, terraced mound in Midway Geyser Basin, not far from the Firehole River, into which it discharges 560 gallons of heated water a minute. The pool is difficult to see because it is so large, the kind of spring whose beauty could be better appreciated from a nearby mountain top. It is also often obscured by clouds of steam that rise from or blow across its surface. Where the pool is deepest, the color of the water appears to be a dark indigo blue; this changes to lighter blues at lesser depths toward the edges of the spring. Surrounding the blue is a ring of emerald green; around that is a yellow ring, which gives way to orange and, finally, red. Each particle of vapor that rises from the surface reflects these colors, so that observed on a sunlit day the spring appears to be covered with steam clouds that are blue, orange, green, and yellow. As General William Tecumseh Sherman wrote of the geyser basins: "In walking among and around them, one feels that in a moment he may break through and be lost in a species of hell."

The upwelling of water in most hot springs is so steady and the overflow so even that the deposits take the form of regular and symmetrical mounds with scalloped edges; or round ridges, like Punchbowl Spring; or broad mounds with gently terraced shoulders, such as those around Grand Prismatic Spring. Conversely, the water from geysers is thrown out violently or scattered by winds, and so the cones of geysers are highly irregular, as Grotto Geyser suggests. After centuries of discharge and deposit, entire geyser basins become floored by siliceous sinter. The flooring can be thin and hence very dangerous when men or beasts wander across it. Siliceous sinter, or geyserite, as some people know it, is a quartzlike mineral similar in many ways to window glass, and frequently as fragile.

In addition to silica, some springs or vents of steam may possess small quantities of carbon dioxide, hydrogen sulfide, arsenic, boron, and fluorine. The Sulfur Cauldron, on the bank of the Yellowstone River, is a boiling yellow pool thick with particles of sulfur, and is acid enough to burn holes in cloth. The Black Dragon's Cauldron seethes like a vat of tar but contains only iron sulfides in the water. Cinder Pool, in the Norris Geyser Basin, resembles hot milk with hollow black buckshot floating on its surface. The metallic-looking globules are not composed of iron, however; they are pellets of nearly pure sulfur that have somehow been manufactured within the depths of the spring. Mammoth Hot Springs, which lie about forty miles north of the edge of the old caldera, are composed of travertine, a form of calcium carbonate. The waters that supply them do not rise up through thousands of feet of rhyolite but rather through subterranean layers of limestone.

Mud Pots

One day spent in this extraordinary landscape gives us puzzles to ponder for a long time. Very little in our previous experience prepares us for Yellowstone's roaring basins. There is too much that is bizarre and incomprehensible, too much that seems like a fantasy that could evaporate as colored vapors. In this state of bewilderment it is a relief to find the mud pots. They at least are familiar, like porridge cooking or corn mush simmering. Here, however, they go to excesses, and every muddy action seems magnified on Yellowstone's scale of hugeness.

Sulfur in the escaping gases combines with water to make sulfuric acid, which decomposes the rhyolites and breaks them down into fine muds. In effect, the pots are springs that are becoming clogged with mud. In many, the bubbling and boiling diminish when the water level recedes in the latter part of summer. Activity at the surface may cease altogether, and all one hears is a coughing deep down in the vent, or perhaps no more than a hiss of steam.

Pink, white, gray, yellow—the colors are always soft pastels, from compounds of sulfur or perhaps of iron, resembling the pots of paint in an artist's workshop, or of clay in a ceramist's studio. Some pots are simple holes in the ground, some are mounds, some are cones built up by viscous blobs of clay, or by pellets flung out in a circle. The clay is not washed away, but rather is worked and reworked hour after hour, year after year.

No two mud pots are alike. The consistency of the mud varies from soup to dry baked clods, and this results in numerous kinds of hurling movements and booming, beeping, bubbling, splashing sounds. The action is particularly attractive to anyone having a camera that can stop the motion with a high-speed shutter. That allows examination of those split seconds when "balloons" of exploding mud are coming apart, or when droplets of mud are flung aloft in forms so fleeting that the human eye can hardly follow them.

If the consistency of the mud is such that it stays in position when thrown up by gases, an infinite number of concentric circles and free-form shapes is produced. Bullets of mud fly in all directions, straight up, obliquely, in arcs, crossfiring out of one pot and into another, and even out of a gray mud vat into a brown one. If a particular point of eruption is kept undisturbed and each burst leaves a concentric ring around the vent, there are soon a hundred concentric rings overlapping and crowding. In material that is especially thick, the expulsions form threads of mud that break into ovoid chunks and scatter in all directions. One grotto produces a platelet of mud about every three seconds, as though it were disgorging coins.

If you stay and listen to mud pot music long enough, you will hear a symphony of hisses, sighs, and puffs played to the background of high-pitched notes from steaming vents. There are drumlike booms, castanet clicks, and spraying wheezes that imitate the sound of a brush against a drum.

The configuration of each throat, or natural mud larynx, together with the consistency of the mud and the degree of the steam explosion, determines the nature of each sound. The rapidity of steam expulsion provides a difference of cadence. Some persons will hear only chaos out of all this, but if you listen carefully there are subtle nuances and accidental rhythms that come as a delightful surprise.

Blobs of mud hurled into the air six feet or so fall back into the vat with a high-pitched splat. Some mud pops with a resonant, echoing sound in wells six or eight feet deep, resulting in a down-to-earth chamber music. A few cavernous grottoes contain little offshoot caves with bubbling vats that sound like several ensembles playing at once. While most of the

Left: Delicate scallops of pearly gray sinter are deposited
along the edge of a Black Sand Basin runoff stream. *Above*: Changing
runoff channels in Black Sand Basin halt advancing
forests of lodgepole pine.

poppings are slow and lazy, there are a few from which the steam comes out furiously, with a spitting that sounds like the frying of eggs. Such places are apt to be named Frying Pan Springs or Sizzling Basin. Deep-throated gurgling is very common, a kind of tympanic sound. In other deep wells the music is that of that famed Guatemalan instrument, the marimba. If an imaginative musician took a stick of lodgepole pine, stood on a baked mud mound, and in his fancy conducted this wild symphony, it would not be the first time man felt inspired by Yellowstone's music.

Changes and Hazards of Hot Springs

The one reliable constant in mud pot music, and in the pots themselves, is change. Yet whether the thermal basins are heating or cooling, the rate is so slow and difficult to detect that for all practical purposes the basins will remain the same for many years to come. There may, of course, be sudden changes, such as those that accompanied or followed the Hebgen Lake earthquake of August, 1959, which had the greatest intensity ever recorded in this part of the Rocky Mountains. The maximum subsidence or sinking of one block of land in relation to another during that earthquake was twenty feet. The shock shook the countryside and unleashed landslides. Geyser basins nearest the center of the earthquake were changed to a marked degree: increased activity, lesser activity, greater or lesser frequency of eruptions, some thermal features made dormant, some clear pools made muddy, and so on.

Such things also happen with the passage of time. Pools may cool or entire thermal basins diminish their action. The ground may also start heating up, and subterranean erosion may undermine the crust of the earth. This can be deceptive and dangerous to animals, man included, where solid-looking ground is not solid at all.

Indeed, every thermal pool is a potential hazard to man and beast. Water snakes, for example, seem not to have evolved enough to distinguish hot water from cold, at least not when they are in a hurry. They are seen on occasion to slither into a boiling pool where, in seconds, their motions stop, and in a very short time they are cooked. Other wild animals also fall into boiling pools. One probable reason for this is that they fail to recognize treacherous ground that is too thin to support their weight. The remains of bison, elk, deer, and other animals are frequently found in the thermal springs; one is named Skeleton Pool for that very reason.

Nor is man much better able to avoid such fatal accidents, and history records a number of occasions during which human beings have had tragic encounters with boiling pools. F. V. Hayden himself broke through and scalded himself up to the knees in hot mud. Others have fallen through crusts with much more serious results. They have stepped off boardwalks and gone in. Although bathing in thermal pools is forbidden, one young man, who thought he was plunging into a pool of moderate temperature, hurled himself into one that measured 178° F. He received second- and third-degree burns over 90 per cent of his body, and a friend rescuing him suffered second-degree burns below the knees. Both were given first aid at Lake Hospital, then flown to the nearest "burn center," nearly four hundred miles away. Several days later the more seriously injured young man died.

The macabre nature of these extremely rare human injuries or fatalities is met by a public reaction out of proportion to their frequency. Safety is a matter of major concern, and the National Park Service is constantly striving to attain better visitor protection without destroying the natural beauty of the thermal areas. Boardwalks themselves are safety features, and railings are furnished where a viewer could inadvertently leave the trail and enter a boiling pool. But the mandate of Congress is to maintain this park in a natural state, and this means no unnecessary railings, and certainly no fences—the antithesis of the national park idea.

Hazards are inherent, of course, in any wilderness —as in any city. Although the agency in charge is

Hot springs choked with fine clay become mud pots; as sources of water diminish, the mud dries out and begins to crack.

responsible for public safety, there must be a point at which each visitor becomes responsible for his actions. Communicating hazard warnings to visitors is an important aspect of the park's public safety effort. If visitors are too young or too old, or in some way unable to recognize the obvious hazards, they should remain under the watchful guidance of other persons. Everything in a national park should be kept natural —including the hazards—and visitors, especially those from urban areas, need to be made aware of the dangers and how to avoid them.

Geysers in Other Lands

The absence of man-made devices around most Yellowstone pools is one of the fundamental reasons why this park is so attractive and popular today. The policy of naturalness, however, does not prevail in all of the world's thermal basins. The famed hot springs of Arkansas were utilized for baths and therapeutic purposes long before Yellowstone's wonders were widely known. A good many other North American hot springs are used as resorts, where people come to relax and bathe. Liard Hot Springs, along the Alaska Highway in British Columbia, Canada, are within a public park, but swimming in them is part of the use of the area. In fact, hot springs are common in nearly all parts of the world, especially in areas of more recent mountain building where subterranean magmatic masses are closer to the surface.

The United States Geological Survey estimates that in the United States alone there is enough heat stored in rocks in the upper six miles of the crust to

equal the heat content of 900 trillion tons of coal. At a time when energy, or the lack of it, is producing numerous crises, one would think that power generated from geothermal resources could be very promising. It may indeed. The United States Geological Survey has inventoried thirteen western states and identified 86 million acres (excluding Yellowstone) as prospectively valuable geothermal resources.

Around the world such resources have already been put to use, and an estimated one million kilowatts is being produced. The most opportune sites are high-powered steam vents that can be capped and put to work. At The Geysers, in northern California (actually fumaroles, or steam vents, rather than geysers), a steam plant is in operation, and the estimated potential production is over 1 million kilowatts.

Italy built the world's first geothermal steam generating plant in the Lardarello area near Florence, and it presently produces over 300,000 kilowatts. In New Zealand, the Wairakei Geothermal Power Project is considered capable of producing about the same amount. It is an impressive experience to stand at the edge of this developed basin and feel the ground vibrating underfoot. The roar is deafening, and even 500 yards away it is almost impossible to hold a conversation. But it is also easy to see the price that has had to be paid in the loss of natural beauty. Great clouds of steam rise from the complex, which is a mass of steamstacks, sheds, pipes, valves, U-joints, superstructures, wire lines, floodlights, bridges, and No Trespassing signs. Nine gigantic conducting pipes carry the steam to a generating plant out of sight beyond distant hills, and along the way can be heard the intermittent pops of steam as automatic valves release the system's surplus energy.

Fortunately, New Zealand has splendid geyser basins that have not been harnessed. This steaming sector is in a belt of great volcanic activity, some twenty miles wide and one hundred fifty miles long, on North Island. There are hot springs, pools, and vents. The basins are replete with sinter terraces, mud pots, explosion pits, gnarled fountains, colorful flats, and geysers that hurl their waters as much as two hundred feet into the air. Like Yellowstone, these areas have been known to modern men for little more than a century. Unlike Yellowstone, there has been a far greater incidence of volcanic violence here in historic times. The Waimangu Geyser, discovered about 1900, became famous for the fact that it flung rocks, mud, and other debris as well as water more than 1,000 feet into the air during eruptions that lasted for several hours and could be heard for miles. In 1903 the geyser killed four persons who had come to see it, and in 1917 it blew itself and the surrounding flat to bits, killing two more persons. The violence seems to have subsided now, and visitors may stroll in peace not only among New Zealand's famous geysers, such as Waipiparangi, Waikorohihi, Te Korokoro o te Taipo, and Mimihomaiterangi, but among remnants of Maori history as well. There are Maori village sites here, and it was Te Heuheu Tukino IV, a Maori chieftain, who donated to the government a nucleus of land that later became Tongariro National Park.

The only other comparable thermal region in the world is in Iceland, where there are about twenty active volcanoes and a thousand hot springs and geysers. The best-known of these features is Great Geysir, which sends a column of hot water 180 feet into the air. Water from naturally heated sources is utilized in indoor swimming pools, greenhouses, homes, and public buildings of Reykjavik, the capital.

In the final analysis, geysers in New Zealand or Iceland or Yellowstone are principally curiosities of nature, their fascination due in some degree to their mystery and rarity. Man, however, must remain little more than a spectator at their performances; if he is to be more than this, and is to know the profound and personal experience that comes from being steeped in the natural ecosystems of Yellowstone, he must go beyond the geysers, into the forest, along the streams, and among the wildlife. He must experience the solitude, feel the wind or rain or snow, or in some way all his own come to understand and appreciate a world of which the thermal features are only a part.

Rising steam escapes in bursts of mud. This constant action grinds the clay into sediment as fine as flour.

5

Of Rivers and Lakes

I have no hesitation in pronouncing the Yellowstone . . . the best trout-fishing stream on earth.

GENERAL WILLIAM TECUMSEH SHERMAN, 1877

Water pouring and seeping from mountain peaks near the upper reaches of Yellowstone's streams supports one of the most extraordinary assemblages of plant and animal life on earth. The forests with their spectacular wildlife are most familiar, but there is also life in the smallest streams, and even in the last place most people would expect to find living organisms: the boiling pools.

Early explorers, of course, had much to say about Yellowstone's aquatic life. They often told how an angler could hook a fish at the edge of Yellowstone Lake, then dip it into a boiling pool on shore and cook it without even taking it off the line. The early scout and trapper Jim Bridger did better than that, or so the legend says. He used to go to a place where hot water supposedly flowed into the lake and, because of its lesser specific gravity, floated in a layer at the surface; he would let his line fall through this heated zone, hook a fish in the cooler waters beneath, and cook it on the way out.

Life in Hot Water

At first sight the steaming springs would appear to be totally uninhabitable. The almost instant death of animals that accidentally enter the pools seems to corroborate this impression. Yet the run-off waters from many a spring contain a progression of life as vivid and visible as colors in a rainbow.

Actually the springs constitute a habitat highly favorable to the growth of algae; there is no reason why algae should not survive, and even thrive, in these thermal environments. Few other ecosystems are as stable as these, even though they are highly fragile. After all, the temperature of the water, its rate of flow, and its quantity are nearly invariable, as close to a "steady state" as nature approaches in the Yellowstone. And, moreover, the springs are remarkably constant in chemical and other properties. Where the waters flowing away from a hot spring have cooled sufficiently to support the growth of algae with orange and yellow pigments, the result is a ring of bright algae around each spring, or along the

Boiling water spills into the Firehole River, Midway Geyser Basin. Brightly colored algae line the edge of the channel where the water has cooled slightly.

streams that leave it. Blue-green algae live in thermal waters up to nearly 170° F. Above that, bacteria are the only form of life. Bacteria do not inhabit all hot springs above this temperature, but in some they grow in filamentous masses of yellow, pink, and white nearly up to the boiling point. These are easily observed by visitors.

In even hotter springs, with temperatures at or above the boiling point, the waters appear to be utterly clear and devoid of any living thing. Yet unbelievable as it seems, life exists in abundance in these boiling pools. Researchers have suspended glass collection slides several feet down in pools with temperatures of over 200° F. (which is above the boiling point at this elevation) and a week later found that filamentous and rod-shaped bacteria had collected on the slides. This occurred in every pool that was tested, and in more than half of the pools the concentration of bacteria formed a film visible to the unaided eye.

Thus, says Dr. Thomas D. Brock, a microbiologist who has done pioneering work in thermal environments, bacteria are able to grow in Yellowstone at any temperature at which there is liquid water, even in pools that are above the boiling point. From these studies it can be concluded that the upper limit for life is not yet known. This opens up the possibility that life existed on earth in primitive boiling pools, perhaps even before the seas, as we know them, were formed. In fact, some rock formations around the world contain fossil microorganisms similar to those in modern thermal springs.

There is no accident about this. Hot water is simply another ecosystem that man has not yet adequately investigated. Dr. Brock feels that these hot environments reveal the extremes to which evolution has been pushed. Organic activity also appears to be many times greater at higher temperatures, and this may mean that the earth's biological potential for productivity is larger than commonly realized. In time man may obtain new light on the origin or transfer of organisms in the universe. It may seem far-fetched, but if life at the boiling point is possible,

then perhaps some forms of interstellar life could survive a fiery entry through the protective atmosphere of planets.

In Yellowstone, all of the heated water that comes up out of the thermal basins departs from those basins in three primary ways. Some goes up in steam and is dissipated in the air. Some flows onto the surrounding ground and sinks. The rest goes into the nearest stream and mingles with waters en route to the sea.

One would think that all this steaming water entering the Firehole River, for example, would eliminate the fish, or certainly trout, which do not relish temperatures much above 75° F. And it does in some streams; Witch Creek, to which the Heart Lake Geyser Basin contributes heated water, is too warm for trout. But the Firehole has so great a volume, and so icy a temperature to begin with, that the warm water flowing into it is soon cooled and thus the fish are not reduced. Quite the contrary, the Firehole is celebrated as one of the best trout-fishing streams in the world. Trout simply stay away from "hot spots" where the steaming streams come in.

Life in Cold Water

In contrast to the heated pools, most of the waters of Yellowstone are very cold indeed, icy at their sources and frozen at least partially in winter. Unlike the "steady state" environments of hot springs, the temperature here varies widely. Water flowing down the streams is reduced in volume during times of freeze-up, and rates of flow are likewise diminished; then during spring, when winter snows melt rapidly, the streams flow swiftly and with increased volume. Hence the organisms that inhabit streams not fed by heated water must endure more variations in temperature and rate of flow than do forms of life in hot springs.

Since aquatic organisms live in an environment for the most part unseen and unfamiliar to man, many persons have looked with approval upon the almost unrestricted killing of fish, even in national parks, and have introduced exotic species simply to provide more

Reflections in an algae-covered pond.

Midway Geyser Basin. Pale yellow bacteria grow in hottest water near the source of thermal activity, but as runoff cools, orange, brown and green algae become established.

variety for fishermen. Yellowstone has eleven species of native fish, but five other species have been introduced, all to satisfy the passion of men for angling. High waterfalls originally prevented the movement of fish upstream. A third of the waters of Yellowstone were therefore devoid of fish; but not any more, for introduced species have survived very well in the upper lakes and streams where food and spawning sites are abundant. Even though stream habitats seem remote, and we can see very little but minnows at first, there is nonetheless a great deal of life.

All of it is dependent, directly or indirectly, upon a mass of tiny organisms. Most basic are the phytoplankton—minute forms of plant life suspended in the water—and other vegetation, and the debris of dead organisms that floats in the lakes or is carried downstream with the dashing currents. Next are the zooplankton, small animal life such as scud and copepods that swim in the water by the millions. All of these plankton are so small that we seldom observe them, except when the phytoplankton experience a "bloom," or population explosion, at which time they become very numerous. If we could gather these and pile them on shore, there would be literally tons of them, visible proof of the substantial biomass that these waters produce.

The lives of nearly all creatures in Yellowstone rivers and lakes are linked at one time or another to this forage. A great many insect larvae live in the waters, ingesting the plankton. Stoneflies, for example, eat algae and diatoms from the rocks as well as bits of wood and bark that come downstream. Immature forms or nymphs emerge from the water in summer and crawl out on the banks. They then transform into flying adults that live but a few days, primarily to mate and lay eggs.

Stoneflies are a major item in the diet of stream fish, but mayflies and caddis flies are also important. Caddis fly larvae build cylindrical cases attached to rocks or aquatic vegetation. The winged adult that emerges resembles a small moth. These gather on rocks and run back and forth or fly over and into the

stream. Dragonflies also hover over rivers and lakes and even hot pools, in which they may become parboiled if they are careless. Inch-long freshwater leeches abound in Yellowstone Lake, seeking out trout to which they can affix their suction-cup mouths. Also in the same lake are fish lice, which attach themselves behind the fins of trout.

The many invertebrates, even in the smallest mountain streams, constitute another link in the chain of life. Fish consume them along with the eggs and young of aquatic animals plus great quantities of terrestrial organisms such as flies, ants, and grasshoppers. Their own eggs and young are likewise food for other species, so that life for fish fry is fraught with dangers. For every thousand eggs deposited, fewer than ten will produce mature trout.

Were it not for all this smaller food, the larger forms of life in Yellowstone rivers and lakes would not survive. Every aspect of this environment is utilized in the natural process of life and death. Each part of this ecosystem, like each part of the human body, has an essential function, and if one part is withdrawn, the whole functions differently or not at all. This is an unseen, unappreciated marvel of a natural region such as Yellowstone. And one of the most striking examples of how all parts of the Yellowstone environment fit together is the circle of life around trout.

The streams and lakes, as we have seen, teem with invertebrate life and algae. Along the edges grow bulrushes and sedges, which extend into lowland marshes. The still waters of lakes and ponds provide ideal environments for several kinds of pondweed, burreed, water milfoil, white water buttercup, and, especially on Isa Lake, the familiar yellow water lily. Trout rely directly and indirectly on aquatic plants and invertebrates, for these are the food of fish like chub, which the trout may devour. Trout also occasionally dine on two kinds of minnows—speckled and longnose dace, which prefer the waters of riffles and rapids —and on mottled sculpins, bizarre-looking fish no more than six inches long, which inhabit fast-flowing streams.

All is not perfectly natural in the trout world, alas, for four of Yellowstone's species of trout are aliens introduced from Europe. Rainbow trout were brought in before the turn of the century and now occupy a considerable number of creeks and rivers in the park. Not only have they intruded into the ecosystem, but they have also interbred with native species to produce hybrids or, more disturbing, pushed original species entirely out of certain localities.

Another trout, the brown, was imported for a reason satisfying to sport fishermen: whereas rainbows spawn in the spring, browns spawn in the fall, extending the angling season. Brown trout live primarily in creeks and rivers and, like the rainbow, have an average weight of one to two pounds.

Brook trout, which are also found in streams and spawn in autumn, are exotic, as are lake trout, or mackinaws, which are more at home in the deep, cold waters of lakes than in streams. Mackinaws are famous for the size they attain; the largest found in Yellowstone, forty-two pounds, was taken from Heart Lake in 1931.

Originally, Yellowstone waters had three native species of the salmon family. All have survived man's attempts to tamper with the aquatic environment, but the brilliantly colored Arctic grayling, a fish usually less than fourteen inches long, cannot endure much competition from other fish. For that reason its distribution and numbers in the park have been reduced; although abundant in two formerly barren lakes at the headwaters of the Gibbon River, and at home in other lakes, it is not among the species that can be taken and kept by anglers. The mountain whitefish, another native, is an occupant of the deeper pools of rivers. But the cutthroat, named for a natural red mark on its jaw, is the fish par excellence in this park, and Yellowstone Lake is its master domain.

The Cutthroat Trout

There is something about this lake, which covers much of the southeast quadrant of the park, that

Gulls on the Molly Islands, in Yellowstone Lake. *Overleaf:* Driftwood and reflections, Yellowstone Lake.

Twilight over Heart Lake.

captures the admiration of men. Even without having a hint of its special nature, they have lavished extraordinary praise on it. Hayden described it as "a vast sheet of quiet water, of a most delicate ultramarine hue, one of the most beautiful scenes I have ever beheld. The entire party were filled with enthusiasm. The great object of all our labors had been reached, and we were amply paid for all our toils. Such a vision is worth a lifetime, and only one of such marvelous beauty will ever greet human eyes."

To some persons the high point here is the drama of wind-whipped waves. To others it is the wintry white expanse of a surface frozen to a depth of three feet. One can cite the reflection of clouds or the glow of a wilderness dawn as reason for cherishing the memory of this wild blue water. Its dimensions are impressive too: it is the largest freshwater lake at such a high elevation in North America, covering 136 square miles and having an average depth of 139 feet.

Yellowstone Lake holds one of the most perfectly functioning aquatic communities remaining on the continent. It is almost self-contained; nothing enters from downstream because the falls of the Yellowstone River are effective barriers. The fish now in it are believed to have entered through a series of streams stretching across the Continental Divide at Two Ocean Pass; they thus moved from the drainage of the Pacific Ocean to that of the Atlantic.

Although there are other fish, such as suckers, in this lake, only one kind of trout—the cutthroat—lives here, and the population must be many millions. Such an abundance has only one meaning to the predatory animals that have come to live near the lake, and that is food. According to some estimates, pelicans, for example, consume about 400,000 cutthroat trout each year. Ospreys dive into the water and can often be seen flying through the air with a trout clutched tightly in their talons. Mergansers, kingfishers, herons, cormorants, terns, and other fish-eating birds also participate in the feast, as do bears, otters, and mink.

The trout would not survive if it were not for an abundance of freshwater shrimp, or the shrimp if there were not an abundance of plankton. Parts of this system, however, may not be very appealing to men who misunderstand their purpose. The trout in Yellowstone Lake and River, wrote the Earl of Dunraven, who traveled through this region in the summer of 1874, "are exceedingly large and fine to look at, and will take a fly or any other sort of bait voraciously; but they are almost useless for food, being with few exceptions full of intestinal insects." The earl did not mean insects. He went on, somewhat more correctly:

The ghosts of digested worms seem to have revenged themselves on the living fish here, for instead of being devoured by the trout, the trout afford food for them. Some people eat these fish, and say that they are very good; but I have never been hungry enough to get over the feeling of repugnance caused by the presence of these parasites. The worms are found, not only in the intestines, but in the solid flesh also; and vary in length and size, the largest being about six inches long. From the scars on the outside of the fish it would seem as if the insects (worms) ate their way completely through them. Occasionally you meet a trout that has escaped the plague, and he is then bright, broad, thick-shouldered, and a very handsome fish; but when the worms are very numerous he becomes a long, lanky, dull-coloured, ugly-looking brute.

This view is that of an explorer and adventurer rather than a scientist, but it is a fair description. The fish tapeworm is common in the Yellowstone River, Heart Lake, and other localities, and an estimated 75 per cent of the fish in Yellowstone Lake are infested with it. The key to its distribution, strange as it may seem, is the presence of birds.

As in any other healthy ecosystem, there is a flow of energy here from one organism to another in a cycle of what-eats-what. In this case, the adult tapeworm lives in such water-frequenting birds as ospreys, gulls, and pelicans. The worms lay their eggs within the birds, and the eggs are in due course flushed away in droppings. When they fall into the waters of a lake or stream, they hatch and are eaten by small crustaceans, a primary food of fish. Once inside the stomach of the fish, young larvae of tapeworm pass through the stomach wall, form cysts, evolve into flatworms, and make their way into the flesh and other parts of the body. This is the worm that human beings usually see. The cycle of life is completed when a worm-ridden fish is eaten by a water bird, after which the tapeworm attaches itself to the intestinal tract of the bird and lays its eggs. From that point another cycle begins.

The fish tapeworm, therefore, is a sign of a healthy ecosystem and the abundance of it in trout does not necessarily mean that something is wrong with the

On mounded nests in marshes, trumpeter swans may raise a brood of up to half a dozen cygnets.

trout. As it stands, cutthroats are the most abundant trout in Yellowstone National Park, occurring in lakes, creeks, and rivers even where they did not occur originally, their range having been extended by man. Alas, the ranges of other fish have also been extended by man, and the ecosystem of Yellowstone Lake, pure as it is, is undergoing changes. The redside shiner, a fish often used as bait, was introduced into the lake in the late 1950's, probably by fishermen. It multiplied rapidly, perhaps too rapidly for the good of the cutthroat trout, because their food habits overlap. Moreover, the shiner may be consuming substantial numbers of juvenile trout that enter the lake from spawning streams. This reduction of incoming fry could have a serious effect on cutthroat populations, and park biologists are keeping a watchful eye on the situation.

The longnose sucker, another species exotic to this lake, may be an additional threat. It occurs by the thousands and spawns every year, whereas the cutthroat spawns only once every two years. The hope is that the cutthroats will remain strong enough, numerous enough, and sufficiently aggressive to keep exotic fish under control.

Fortunately, the effect of angling by human beings can be reduced when necessary. Cutthroat numbers, though great, are not inexhaustible. Some time ago, creel censuses and other surveys showed that the numbers of trout had begun to decline, whereupon the National Park Service instituted regulations designed to lower the number of fish removed from the lake. Ultimately, further restrictions may have to be added, then catch-and-release fishing only, and possibly after that—no fishing at all by men. This would at least restore a portion of the original wildness, where the only predators the trout had to avoid were native mammals and birds.

The Wandering Pelicans

The lives of birds are subtly linked with those of cutthroat trout. Like nearly all large-sized migratory species, white pelicans have suffered from encroach-ment by man upon the wild isolation needed by birds at nesting time. Through the years, therefore, they established rookeries as far from the dangers of man and beast as possible. For example, in the southeast arm of Yellowstone Lake are two scraps of land called the Molly Islands. They are not much to nest on. Their combined areas equal scarcely an acre. One is called Rocky and the other Sandy, both names descriptive and justified. Scant greenery graces these specks of land—a few clumps of willow, some cinquefoil, and a generous quantity of stinging nettle. Most of the year they are covered with ice and snow.

Inhospitable as this may seem, the wandering pelicans arrive as early as April, following the melting of ice, and endure the vagaries of a blustery spring in order to reproduce. They find in the Molly Islands that one requisite denied them in most other places: remoteness. Indeed, this is the only white pelican breeding colony in a national park and the last one in Wyoming.

The birds pay little attention to nest preparation; sticks and stones appear to suffice, and the result is more of a scrape than a nest. Far more important is how much attention the parents pay to the young when hatched, for perils threaten even here in Yellowstone Lake. June nights can be brutally cold for neglected young; water is hazardous to featherless chicks; there is always the possibility of predation, perhaps by swimming mammals or swooping hawks; and diseases are common among the young of all animals. Moreover, the neighbors have to be watched: three other species of birds—California gull, double-crested cormorant, and Caspian tern—nest on these islands. Of five hundred eggs that may be laid, scarcely a hundred young pelicans will hatch and grow to adulthood.

After three or four weeks of helplessness, the young begin to wander around their island home, gathering into groups called pods. In August they fly for the first time, and in September they begin their fall migration. Through recoveries of banded birds it has been discovered that most pelicans from the Molly

Islands travel through the southwestern United States and winter along the Pacific Coast of Mexico.

All this is easy to simplify on paper, but the coming, nesting, and going of pelicans is actually a complex, delicately balanced operation. If any part were eliminated the whole cycle might be affected. Should the pelicans be persecuted and become too wrought up to reproduce, they might abandon the islands. That would weaken a link in the chain of bird–tapeworm–trout, and if the cutthroat, which is probably more parasitized than any other trout in the Rocky Mountains, were to be freed or partly freed of its parasites, what then? There is no point in speculating further, because such events are unlikely to happen in Yellowstone, even though the natural regimen of lakes elsewhere has been altered when the ecosystem was disrupted.

Natural Aquatic Systems

Altogether, the remarkable functioning of this aquatic system is so intricate and interrelated that man is only just beginning to understand it. Whether he can get rid of the exotic fish in Yellowstone Lake and restore the lake to its original balance is an open question. But all is not lost. In the south arm of the lake, which is eight miles long, the fish fauna remains more or less as it was originally, with about the same number of cutthroats, the equivalent age and size relationships, and with very few exotic fishes yet spread to that area. Perhaps by studying that small portion of the lake man can find a way to let the cutthroats themselves reduce the numbers of intruders.

In any event, many years will be required before the aquatic ecosystems can be brought back to their original balance. Until recent years the term "maximum sustained yield" guided fishery management, and for nearly a century the policy was to stock park waters with hatchery-reared fish and to provide the limit of fish for as many anglers as possible. But park authorities came to realize that sustained yield is an agricultural term, and that insofar as it applies to any kind of wildlife it has no place in a national park. The policy now is to provide high quality angling for wild fish in natural environments. Angling for hatchery fish can be enjoyed in streams outside park boundaries.

There is another threat in increased angling. Even if catch-and-release fishing were established in Yellowstone, a great influx of fishermen would be detrimental to stream banks and lake shores, which already show signs of erosion from overuse. In one recent year, between July 15 and September 1, 45,000 anglers fished along seven miles of the Yellowstone River below Yellowstone Lake. Just downstream from there the river is closed to angling—and it is one of the best places in the park to see waterfowl, moose, bison, and other forms of life. This is a superior wildlife habitat and the absence of intrusion by fishermen helps to keep it that way.

Park biologists believe that man can derive a vast amount of satisfaction from the aquatic habitat with little or no damage to the ecosystem. If so, more disciplines than ichthyology will be needed to manage the aquatic habitats. One interesting trend is the growing visitor interest in simply watching fish swim naturally in undisturbed and unpolluted streams. Cutthroat spawning runs, for example, have excited a great deal of attention among visitors to Yellowstone. This raises again the question of what a national park should be. In other places sport fishing is enjoyed for its own sake, and certain public lands are managed to produce a maximum opportunity for enjoyment of angling. Here the natural resources, including all wildlife populations, are conserved in ecosystems as little altered as possible, and are managed to produce opportunities for human appreciation of nature.

Pelicans and young on Molly Islands, Yellowstone Lake.

6

Among the Lodgepoles

The sleep-giving, soothing fragrance of the resinous pine, cleanest, sweetest and most healing of all scents, fills the air.

EARL OF DUNRAVEN,
The Great Divide, 1874

The more we left the familiar places of Yellowstone and went into the interior of the park the more we were struck by the number of phenomena that, in their way, are as fascinating as geysers and as puzzling as life in hot springs. It is entirely possible to spend an interesting summer solely along the terraces beside the rivers, because there, where moisture lingers longest, an abundance of plant and animal life exists. So thick a mat of vegetation has grown that we not only cannot see the soil but must dig through six inches of rotting stems and leaves to find it.

Sedges densely cover the lowlands. Wild rye grows higher than one's head, a richness reminiscent of Africa. Certain species that grow in drier places are also here: thistle, aster, yampa, dock, and yarrow. As we walk—or sometimes force our way—through this grassland, we also observe some of the animal life associated with it. Elk graze near the river. Butterflies feed on the flowers. Dragonflies sweep across the meadows. We come upon a pile of fur and bone, evidence of a grizzly feast the previous spring.

Suddenly a special odor, both pungent and sweet, is sensed. For a moment we are bewildered by this new fragrance and do not recognize it. Then, as we draw closer, the bewilderment fades; we have walked into a patch of wild spearmint. Kneeling, we see that our boots have crushed some leaves, and so we and the meadows are redolent with the scent of mint. It lingers for a while and eventually disappears, but the memory of so unexpectedly finding it endures.

The sun burns into these low moist meadows with a high intensity, and it is a relief to climb to higher, drier, and cooler places. Engulfed by lodgepole pines, we feel a sense of relief at finding ourselves in a more familiar environment than that of the aquatic or thermal systems below. The air is filled with scents of flowers and the sharpened resinous tang of conifers. Here, as we give ourselves to the moods of wind and music and shadows, as we hear the muffled call of a jay higher up on a ridge or the hammering of a woodpecker, we expect to recognize and comprehend most of what we see. Yet for all its familiarity the lodgepole forest has more mysteries than we imagined.

Lodgepoles of uniform age often grow so closely together as to resemble a stockade wall.

For one thing, it resembles the forests of the Pacific Northwest more than any other, which seems rather strange when the prevailing wind direction for the transport of seeds and pollen is from the southwest. Botanists, however, are beginning to find some hints of how this came about. Fifteen thousand years ago there were no lodgepoles here. In fact, there was little or no vegetation at all; the glaciers had swept away earlier growth and covered the land with a mantle of ice. As climates warmed and the ice age ended, earth was exposed once more and alpine species of plants took root, the winds very likely carrying in seeds that germinated at the fronts of receding glaciers. Conditions probably were analogous to those in Glacier Bay, Alaska, today, where mats of lichens and avens commence a long succession of vegetation as soon as the glaciers melt.

Seeds reaching Yellowstone evidently did come on prevailing winds from the southwest, the direction of the Snake River Plain. Only species existing on that plain at that time were in a position to reach Yellowstone, and those species had somehow come from the Northwest. So the Snake River Plain served, in effect, as a transfer point for plants spreading to Yellowstone. This might seem like a roundabout way for the plateaus to be vegetated, but evidence deciphered from bog and lake bottom deposits shows that following the introduction of alpine plants came dwarf birch, cottonwood, whitebark pine, Engelmann spruce, and alpine fir—all typical of the Pacific Northwest.

Though the number of species involved in this transfer was relatively small and the story is not by any means thoroughly proved, it raises the issue of where Yellowstone vegetation did originate and what will happen to it during the coming 15,000 years. No one knows the answer to either question. Lest we assume that the forest stands eternal, however, it is wise to observe that the entire Yellowstone flora has developed its own characteristics, which are changing continuously. From the roads or trails anyone can notice readily the general characteristics of the woods and swamps and prairies, but a perceptive hiker sees much more: a meadow obviously opened years ago by fire, a cluster of fallen logs all pointed in the same direction as though hurled there by wind or avalanche, the invading vegetation that follows the death of a thermal basin.

Indeed it is these subtleties that open to the hiker's mind and eye not one Yellowstone but hundreds: Yellowstones of the past, whose evidence is all about him; Yellowstones of the present, whose changes are occurring every minute—perhaps nearly imperceptibly; and Yellowstones of the future, about which he can speculate on the basis of observations. He walks not in a landscape ruined or badly altered by man but in a natural ecosystem that is constantly changing from the original past to the age of tomorrow.

In Primeval Woods

After the glaciers had melted from primitive Yellowstone, a warm, dry period commenced. Botanists call this the altithermal, deducing its existence by examination of pollen in bog deposits and inferring that the warm climate caused coniferous forests to diminish. When that happened, the area of sagebrush grassland expanded.

Today the dry, hot period is fading and the altithermal is being replaced by cooler and wetter times. The grassland is no longer expanding; plants adapted to warmer climates and formerly found at high elevations now grow in lower places. Sagebrush, limber pine, and Douglas fir have almost vanished from around Yellowstone Lake, and the spruce may well be spreading again.

This shift from dry to wet must have begun rather rapidly, since pollen deposits show an outburst of spruce activity. It may also have brought opportune conditions for the growth of aspen, which is found today primarily between grasslands and coniferous forests. Sagebrush has continued to hold its own against the advancing woods, however, because it produces abundant seeds and thrives under a variety of conditions. Near the sagebrush here and there on

A healthy lodgepole pine community shows signs of growth,
decay and enrichment.

drier, steppe-like sites grow lupine, yarrow, needle-grass, and wheatgrass.

But open grasslands and sage-covered slopes do not predominate; 80 per cent of Yellowstone National Park is forested. And 80 per cent of the forest is lodge-pole pine. One of the reasons that lodgepole is king of the forest is the paucity of other species of trees. While tropical forests may have nearly three hundred species of trees, Yellowstone has only eleven, seven of which are conifers: lodgepole, whitebark, and limber pines, subalpine fir, Douglas fir, Engelmann spruce, and Rocky Mountain juniper. At first glance, one would think that they were scattered helter-skelter across the landscape, but there is in fact a remarkable organization to their distribution; their location is far from being a matter of chance. Latitude is one factor; if the Yellowstone region were just 15° farther south it would fall in a belt of natural deserts that surrounds the earth at more or less 30° latitude. That would make the climate drier and the wet and dry seasons distinct. Instead, Yellowstone's precipitation falls fairly uniformly throughout the year, with perhaps a little more moisture in June. The vegetation is not dried out periodically, as in California, or wetted so heavily in summer, as in Minnesota. Of prime importance, even in the desert, is not how much rain falls but when; that is, whether the moisture is available to roots at a time when the plants can use it.

Yellowstone soils tend to be generally moist through the growing season; snow melt soaks the ground in spring, followed by an inch of rain in July and another in August, most of it evenly spread. Still there are differences. Climatic and other conditions account for more moisture in some parts of the park than in others; the annual precipitation in the Lamar Valley is fourteen inches, and in the Bechler area thirty-eight inches. In addition, rain that falls on south-facing slopes, which receive more sunlight, tends to run off or evaporate and thus does not sink in as much as on north-facing slopes. Thus there is heavier growth of forests on north-facing slopes, a contrast that is often a striking feature of Yellowstone landscapes.

Another factor influencing plant distribution is snow, and since heavy accumulations cling to higher slopes until well into June, altitude itself also makes a difference; only species adapted to the burden of heavy snow or the rigors of high country living—species such as whitebark pine and subalpine fir—can manage to survive. Prevailing wind direction also plays an important part in the placement of plants, and the effect of storms is substantial, especially those in summer that are accompanied by lightning and sweep across the plateaus, leaving forest fires behind.

Fire and Lodgepole Pine

Lightning and fire, of course, have been occurring since glacial times, and one species of tree in particular, the lodgepole pine, has profited from them more than any other, probably because of its serotinous cones. Such cones are normally tightly closed until they reach a temperature of 140° or so, as would occur in a forest fire. The cones then open and the seeds are released and dispersed. Lodgepoles therefore must have thrived and spread where competing plants were destroyed by fire.

Whether lodgepoles finally became the dominant Yellowstone pine in exactly this manner is not known, although it seems fair to assume that the present distribution is a result of a long evolution of trees advancing into burned-over areas and thriving there. But this brings us to another of Yellowstone's forest mysteries, for unlike lodgepoles growing elsewhere, most of those in Yellowstone today do not have serotinous cones. Their cones open at maturity and the seeds disperse in the year they are produced.

This may seem to be a sort of backward evolution. But the answer may be relatively simple: lodgepoles here no longer need closed cones. According to one theory, they have spread so widely and thickly on the main plateaus that they have eliminated many competing trees, such as the easily burned spruce and fir. Without the high spires of spruce and fir to attract lightning, it may be that fewer fires get started.

If this is indeed a reason why lodgepoles have in-

In the Yellowstone region, sagebrush and aspen are relics from former times when the climate was warmer. *Overleaf*: The sloping vales on Mount Washburn contain blue lupines and glacier-deposited boulders.

creased in Yellowstone, and if they catch fire only every century at most, it is not surprising that trees with serotinous cones have been replaced by trees with open cones. Without fires, the pines with serotinous cones could not reproduce, while those that open their cones spread abundantly. The lodgepole pine therefore seems to have shifted from one genotype to another and thereby been able to hold its dominance.

At a casual glance, Yellowstone appears to consist of hundreds of square miles of unadulterated lodgepole pine forests. But the purity is not as widespread as it looks. For a reason not well understood, young whitebark pines are often scattered among the lodgepoles. This is puzzling for several reasons. The whitebark is believed to be rather intolerant of other species. It is said not to do particularly well in shade. And seemingly so few whitebarks ever reach maturity in the lodgepole forest that the parent seed source remains a mystery. It is hard to explain why the young trees are here in such abundance.

Still, the lodgepole has little competition. Without other fire-tolerant species—yew, larch, white pine— it has spread with ease in a variety of forest sites, as well as to places where trees have difficulty growing: thermal areas, wet sedge and grass meadows, dry steppes, and sandy soils. The real question is whether lodgepoles are only transitional and will someday yield to other species. Apparently not. Analyses of present stands show lodgepoles replacing lodgepoles. There seems to be no tendency for Douglas fir to assume command, as it does in much of the Northwest. Spruce and fir are hardy and tolerant of shade, and at higher elevations they do come up through lodgepole and survive; for the present, however, they do not survive to the exclusion of lodgepole, and a pure stand of spruce-fir is hard to find in Yellowstone forests. If lodgepole should get shouldered aside, a dry, hot year with forest fires might be enough to take out the spruce and bring back the lodgepole.

In another mystery of these woods, the widely distributed ponderosa pine has never been found in Yellowstone. This pine thrives in all of the western states. But apparently it never occurred on the Snake River Plain—it is not there even now—and thus was never in a position to enter Yellowstone, even though the park has some good ecological niches for ponderosa.

Had the national park idea not developed here so long ago, we could not as neatly speculate, or puzzle over, the truths and mysteries of all these trees. This rare and priceless ecosystem has been held intact and never commercially logged, an island of wilderness in a sea of cultivated crops.

A Gathering of Insects

Even as forceful an idea as a national park free of man's influence has had its setbacks. Man could not allow anything that seemed, in his view, a threat to the existence of these magnificent forests. And so for decades the thesis was generally accepted that "harmful" insects had no place in wild forests, not even in national parks, and man assumed that when the forest became "diseased" something had to be done to excise this malignance.

"Miracle," however, would be a better word than "malignance" for the mountain pine beetle, which has been a native in Yellowstone forests for centuries and has evolved as an integral part of the ecosystem. In July the female seeks out a sturdy and vigorous pine with a thick enough inner bark to give good home and sustenance for her brood. She bores into the bark and becomes surrounded by a flow of resin. As she feeds, the resin passes through her gut and is oxidized into a sex-attracting substance analogous to a hormone. The total production may be minuscule, but any male perceiving it is obliged, literally obliged, to come to the tree and enter her gallery.

In addition to being a sex attractant, this chemical is also an aggregant. When perceived by other females, they too are obliged to go to the tree, and what follows is a mass attack. Hundreds of beetle pairs will riddle a tree's defense and dissipate its flow of resin so much that it cannot sustain its original vigor. The

Pronghorns prefer open plains and slopes, a necessity for the fastest
land mammal in the Western Hemisphere.

Tall grasses are bent by mountain breezes at the edge of the
Lamar River Valley.

beetle also brings a fungus that further shatters the tree's resistance. All this may take several weeks, but with hundreds, perhaps even thousands, of beetles attacking, the tree eventually dies.

Although this may produce a shocking vision of beetles obliterating the forest entirely, the fact is that they do not. Young trees have thin inner bark that does not provide a suitable home for the beetles; the more young trees come to predominate, therefore, the more the insect population declines and fades away. Hence, the thinning out of older trees by beetles is beneficial to the young trees left. In national forests outside the park, mature trees are logged before the beetle can get to them, and logging operations may come directly to the park boundary; yet the forest in time grows back. Formerly there might have been considerable agitation for park authorities to control the pine beetles, but now foresters seem to understand and appreciate the park policy of letting native infestations run their course and be observed as part of the natural scene.

This understanding is partly due to man's new awareness that there is little he can do about the beetle anyway. He can log off all the trees elsewhere, but not in national parks. His use of harmful pesticides is being discontinued. And his state of knowledge regarding animal behavior is still very primitive. So in Yellowstone we watch the course of the beetle's progress with a fresh appreciation of the ways of nature.

At this writing there are hordes of beetles in the Bechler region, and a great many trees are being killed. But there is no cause for alarm, and the beetles are not expected to spread. In forty years of recorded entomological history, these beetles have never seriously infested lodgepoles on the higher plateaus, perhaps because the winters are too severe. Of course, we cannot expect the situation to continue unchanged; in fact, beetles have lately managed to fly up and become established in a few trees on the plateau. Perhaps they have been flying up there intermittently for centuries. Whether they survive for long and, if so,

increase to substantial numbers, is a question only time can answer. At least in a national park, where beetles are as precious as orchids, and as much a part of the natural fauna as bears and elk, there is reasonable assurance that the altering hand of man will be stayed.

Thus the forests of Yellowstone are accruing greater value as time goes on. Botanists are impressed with the ways in which the lodgepole pine has adapted to and conquered its environment quite as capably as sequoias that have lived for four thousand years. Today lodgepole is still well adapted and covers an extensive territory here. Eventually, these wild woods may stand in high contrast to managed forests outside the park.

Another theory being questioned is that the more man prevents forest fires, the more dead and down material will accumulate under the trees; therefore, when a fire does start it will burn hotter, spread farther, and do more damage than any fire before it, thus ruining the ecosystem. But observations do not seem to support this theory, at least in Yellowstone's lodgepole forests. In fact, there may be no especially great accumulation of debris at all. Logs rot here at a rate of approximately 1 per cent each year, and the rate of decay for all forest products seems to equal the rate of accumulation. Yellowstone has a wide representation of native insects and other types of wood and litter consumers, and what we perceive taking place today must have gone on for centuries before man came and altered the natural fire regime. The only exotic plant disease is white pine blister rust. Otherwise, Yellowstone's ecology is native; insects feeding on vigorous trees are followed by those that feed on dead trees; and the insects in turn have predators that feed on them.

Hiker's Paradise

The forests of Yellowstone National Park contain, of course, far more than trees and mountain pine beetles. A hiker discovers this sooner than anyone else because he enters the depths of the forests or the distant meadows, where animals that needed to escape the enclaves of cars and people have settled in quiet places. When he straps on his pack and takes off into the woods, he exposes himself to some of Yellowstone's greatest adventures.

He follows a steep rough trail, but the rocks that get in his way or the roots that trip him are scarcely noticed. He is attuned to a plane of interest above which such irritations cannot distract. What captures his attention instead are scenes like serene and quiet lakes where swallows swoop down to the surface to drink. These birds are as important to the universe as he is, and he watches them for a while. From the point where each scoops water a widening ripple dissolves the surface into fragments of forest and sky that roll back and forth in a liquid blue mirror. Each split second of this tableau is an instant abstract painting that flashes into view and then vanishes.

Along the trail he meets some artists who are attempting with canvases, palettes, and brushes to capture these scenes on their own terms and with their own talents. It is not uncommon to find artists doing this in Yellowstone; in fact, a major function of the park is to preserve a landscape completely uncluttered so that they, or a hiker, or anyone else can see it in his own way, in his own time, to his own satisfaction.

The hiker may go wherever he wishes, with or without a schedule, with or without a goal. He may climb completely out of the lodgepole forest, up to the highest limits of life, where little but lichens grow on the mountain peaks. There he may pause to marvel at the tenacity of life, where mosses establish themselves in bits of wind-blown dust caught in rocks. As mats of moss develop, more soil and nourishing organic materials are formed, after which the avens and a host of other species follow in succession.

Coming down from the peaks, he tramps across alpine and subalpine meadows, through spruce-fir forests that begin at a tree line of about 9,600 feet, and returns to the lodgepole community. Lodgepoles spread far and wide across the main plateaus and to some there is a certain monotony and sameness in so

much of it. Not to him. He sees no monotony in Yellowstone. If there is not a meadow to explore, then there is a copse of Douglas fir, or a hillside of sagebrush, or a clone of aspen.

The artist within him may consider aspen more exciting than any tree; its bark is often broken or chewed by elk into a crossword puzzle pattern of black and white. Or the trunk may be utterly smooth and unblemished. Some trunks are graced with folds, or embossed with odd-shaped lumps, or adorned with undulating ridges, all touched with quivering shadows cast by the leaves above. Each leaf itself may present an almost runic alphabet of designs left by insect miners.

Everywhere the hiker finds artistic, sculptural, and architectural values—downed logs, gnarled roots, old knots, twisted limbs and trunks. Two eyes and a brain are not enough to record and absorb what is here; he takes many pictures and perhaps tapes a few sounds to help retain impressions. But there are vivid experiences or breathtaking surprises that no camera can photograph. That is why he cannot tell others, or even explain with pictures, the meanings of some of his most profound experiences.

He hikes beneath lava cliffs on which pines perch like sentinels, then threads his way across a gray rock slide. At the head of a canyon he comes to a roaring alcove where water slides out of the lodgepole woods and arcs from the edge of a ledge into space. Spray swirls up and soaks him while he examines a prize at the chasm edge: a dripping cluster of flowers with petals of white and yellow and green. He had found these before in shadowy glades or quiet bogs—a grass-of-parnassus, whose floral form has never ceased to delight him.

Return to the Wild

The hiker may cross a wide plateau where there is little moisture, and so is thirsty when he kneels at a tiny creek on the other side. It plays for him the softest and most delicate music, lightly splashing with bell-like sounds, washing against the moss with a swish, or falling rhythmically into a tiny pool. The sweep of grandeur in Yellowstone is not all on a mountain scale; life in and around these pools, or on old logs, occurs in shapes and forms he may never have seen before, and reminds him to look for glimpses of natural life in similar niches back home.

This park has such a diversity of habitats that more than a thousand species of flowering plants have been found in it so far. If he looks in the proper places he can find a few of them: orchids in bogs and ravines; buttercups in moist vales; roses and raspberries in rocky gardens; kinnikinnick on the ground in lodge-

Aspen leaves transform to shimmering gold in late September.

pole glens; bearberry, blueberry, whortleberry in varied environments. There are also deadly poisonous plants such as water hemlock, and fascinating ones like tiny sundews, which capture insects with their sticky pads and absorb them with protein-digesting enzymes.

Each of these is part of a world the hiker may not understand completely, where currents and rhythms of growth and decay belong to a universe about which no man knows all there is to know. He cannot solve every riddle he sees, but he reads the trail as he does a book and gets more glimpses of creation than he did back in the shelter of civilization.

Other trails lead away from the one he follows. He is tempted to take each one and hike all night if necessary, so that no vale is missed or meadow passed without his knowing its grace and charm. He wants to cast off the chains that bind him to returning, and stay here for as long as this perfection lasts.

He may lie in thick rich grass beneath the lodgepole pines. An overhang draped with curtains of grass tempts him to climb to the base of a cliff. Or out of curiosity he will try to follow a streamlet hidden by sedge. He watches the heads of sage and grass dance gently in the air. An old patriarchal lodgepole stands alone in the meadow, abandoned by its neighbors that perhaps burned away in a fire that left only it to survive.

A hiker finds in Yellowstone National Park the simple, unforgettable refreshment of looking into a tumbling stream of clean, free water, or up into the open sky. The sky has a special importance. Elsewhere he took it for granted; it had little meaning. Now it shines with an all-encompassing blue he seldom sees elsewhere. It and the sun give light to everything; its blue caresses all other colors. It contains both movement and life—the clouds and bats and birds—receives the tips of trees, engulfs the steam from thermal basins. It is busy, yet silent. The look of it heralds the weather, at least for the next few hours; the sky

brings a thousand moods—of bright white light, of swirling storms, of sunset colors. And at times he simply sits and watches the clouds as they drift and change. No medium he knows transfers him so quickly into the restlessness of time. All Yellowstone is restless, dynamic, changing. It has always changed. Once there were clouds of fire and ash. Once there were walls of ice. Once many centuries ago a man much like himself might have crawled up on this very ridge in search of bison. . . .

The hiker's time grows short. One final memory is that of a sunlit canyon in later afternoon, a pageant of light and form and movement. Each minute the colors and shadows change. A pine on a pinnacle alters from green to orange to purple. Each ledge is converted by shadows into bas-reliefs, which flatten with the gray and black of evening. Some ridge tops stand out as though suspended in space; some coalesce in a herringbone pattern of brown and orange and yellow.

A chill wind rises from below the rim. Around him the wind sings high and low choral notes through lodgepole limbs, and he listens until almost the last of the light is gone. The music goes on, and will play all night; the wolves and owls will hear it, as he has heard it on nights before in the wilderness, only now he has stayed to the limit of his time.

He goes, refreshed, equipped with a new supply of zest, relaxed, at peace. Someday he will return, compelled by some unceasing call he cannot define. He will repeat in his dreams these moments of reality he knew, and will set in motion preparations for the day when he comes back to the park.

His return will be a moment hoped for, worked for, planned for. He will come to the head of the trail, breathe deeply of the pine-scented air, strap on his pack, and go once again among the lodgepoles. In there somewhere, or perhaps on a high peaked ridge in the distance, he will let the immensity of Yellowstone bring him down to the size of a man.

Lodgepole pines are tall and stately but not always sturdy, and are easily felled by wind, avalanche or insects.

7

Grizzly Country

There seems to be a tacit assumption that if grizzlies survive in Canada and Alaska, that is good enough. It is not good enough for me. . . . Relegating grizzlies to Alaska is about like relegating happiness to heaven; one may never get there.

ALDO LEOPOLD,
A Sand County Almanac, 1949

In a sense, Yellowstone belongs to the grizzly bear. Not the black bear or the elk or the moose or bison. The latter are parts of the ecosystem and as important to it as limbs are to a tree. But the grizzly shares the upper portion of the pyramid of life with few other mammals and is widely respected, though certain species, such as the bison, appear to be indifferent when a grizzly is near.

Man more than respects the grizzly; he sees in this mammal a symbol of the original wilderness and of man's success in saving part of the life system in which the grizzly evolved. That evolution has been taking place here ever since the melting of the great ice sheet that once covered most of the region, and the grizzly, along with the bison, represents in many ways the essence of primitive America.

The Role of the Bear

Huge and powerful though the grizzly may be, it did not attain its important place in the pyramid of life just by threatening its neighbors. That pyramid is a collection of interrelated energy systems, at the base of which are plants that convert solar energy and soil nutrients into living organic matter. Whatever animals have evolved in this region or entered it from the outside have had to adapt to the available food and living space. This necessity prevails in all parts of the ecosystem, in lakes where freshwater shrimp live on algae, in meadows where rodents exist on seeds and leafy greens, in the sky where insectivorous birds make sweeps for invertebrate life, and in the several environments where grizzlies consume both plants and animals. In Yellowstone the most visible occupants of the middle tier of the pyramid of life are the herds of ungulates—bison, deer, moose, pronghorn, bighorn, and elk—who together consume immense quantities of leaves, twigs, stems, and sometimes entire plants. They often favor some plant species over others, resulting in a substantial impact upon the make-up and condition of vegetation in the park.

Then there are the carnivores, which depend on

Grizzly bears in Hayden Valley.

plants only indirectly. Badgers consume ground squirrels, which in turn eat seeds or grass. Cutthroat trout and grayling depend on freshwater shrimp, while ospreys, pelicans, and bald eagles feed on the trout. And finally the impressive large predators—coyote, wolf, mountain lion, and grizzly bear—feed on lesser animals. The grizzly eats both vegetation and animal life.

As we near the apex of this complex ecological pyramid of life, there is a great reduction in the number of species and the number of individuals. Biologists at Isle Royale National Park, in Michigan, found that in one year it takes 100,000 pounds of plant food, mainly shrubs, to produce 6,000 pounds of moose, which in turn support only 100 pounds of wolf. We do not know exactly what it takes in terms of plant and animal life to sustain a 600-pound grizzly, but the tonnage must be enormous; it is safe to assume that a great deal of wild land, free from man's disruption, is required.

The grizzly is obviously well equipped to sustain its position of eminence in the Yellowstone pyramid. No study that we know of has measured the force exerted by its jaws in biting or its paws and claws in slapping, but there is sufficient energy in both actions to destroy nearly any animal swiftly. The claws can extend over five inches from the toes and are sharp enough to act as knives in tearing the toughest hide. Their principal use is for digging, and many hours are spent by the grizzly rolling back tough sod in search of tender roots and insect grubs, and in tearing apart rotten logs to feast on ants, beetles, and related invertebrates. Nevertheless, the grizzly is strong enough to handle nearly any demand for offense or defense. Only in a few other animals, such as the rhino and the tiger, has nature developed such an awesome combination of speed and power.

Grizzlies have not evolved the depth of vision needed by most of the large vegetarians that depend on flight to escape enemies, and so they are unable to distinguish objects far away. Neither are they adept at discerning stationary objects. But their hearing is excellent and their sense of smell is equivalent to that of dogs, to which they are distantly related.

It is easy to assume on observing such a ponderous creature that the animal is slow and its movements sluggish. No belief about this bear could be more dangerous for a man confronting a grizzly in the wilderness. At such a time a man needs to make some quick and very accurate calculations as to whether or not to run. If he runs he is almost sure to release in the bear an inherent tendency to pursue. Once running, a man can only hope that he is much, much closer to a tree than to the grizzly, for he needs not only sufficient time to reach the tree but to climb at least twelve feet up in it. The bear probably will not come after him unless the structure of the lower branches is conducive to climbing. Yet grizzlies have reached up into trees and pulled men down. Most of all, it is crucial to keep in mind the fact that grizzlies can run at thirty miles an hour and men cannot.

Fortunately, such encounters are extremely rare and usually involve only one bear at a time. In the last hundred years, in all North American national parks, there have been only five human fatalities attributed to grizzlies. Mating takes place in June, and except for joint feeding on grass, roots, berries, and carcasses, that is about the only time adult bears ever associate with each other. For the most part the male is a solitary animal, and so is the female, unless she possesses cubs. Grizzlies do not roam about—or attack—in packs.

The Life of the Grizzly

Emerging from their dens in late March and April, grizzlies are ravenous, and they arrive upon the scene at a time most propitious for satisfying their hunger. They have slept through the winter, expending only a minimum of energy, while moose, deer, and elk battled snow and cold and contended with a dwindling food supply. Early spring is a most difficult and critical time of existence for these ungulates, and the grizzlies take advantage of it.

While snow on the higher plateaus remains deeply

The omnivorous black bear finds in Yellowstone an ample supply
of wild foods to maintain its enormous bulk.

The coyote and other predators feed upon small animals.

packed and usually crusted over, the warmth of spring begins to melt away snow in the valley bottoms. Meadows along the Gibbon, Madison, and Firehole rivers are released from their snow cover, and groups of elk are attracted to the newly exposed grasses and sedges that remain from last year's growing season.

Elk that survive the winter with at least some reserves of energy are alert as always to the possibility of a grizzly attack; they will be spared. But a few, such as those that made poor choices on where to spend the winter, may not have built up enough fat reserves to tide them over. This applies especially to the very young and the very old, which may be in a state of debilitation. They are thus targets for marauding grizzlies.

Working alone or in pairs, grizzlies harass elk by chasing them at an easy lope. At a crucial moment the bear can put on an impressive burst of speed to capture an elk that lags behind or to split one off from the herd. If an elk lacks sufficient energy to escape, the grizzly may simply walk up, pull it down, and dispatch it, but the process is not always so easy. To pull down a slow-running elk the grizzly rears on its hind legs, grasps the animal on or over the rump, and allows its weight to collapse the elk's hind quarters. After this it shakes and breaks the victim's neck with its jaws.

Grizzly predation on elk is not a major influence in regulating the numbers of elk, for a total of only about 250 grizzlies live in the park, and only during spring is their diet predominantly the flesh of elk and other ungulates. But grizzly predation, in addition to that of the rare mountain lion and wolf, does assist in sustaining the quality of the ungulates: the less healthy animals are culled from the herd. Individuals in better physical condition survive predation and the rigors of winter; they will produce the next generation, thus maintaining vitality of the species.

During the rest of the year, attacking prey is not usual for grizzlies, or their principal method of getting food. They are scavengers and opportunists and will take whatever edibles they come upon, including carcasses, berries, roots, mice, and ground squirrels. During late summer and autumn they cannot rely on elk for food because elk are in their prime and stragglers are harder to find. So grizzlies tear up the ground for roots and bulbs and carry on diligent quests for the bulbous stems of melica and other grasses. Thus most of the year they are predominantly vegetarians and search assiduously for leaves, twigs, fruit, and nuts.

To observe a grizzly mother and her cubs on a morning prowl for food is one of the tremendous sights of Yellowstone country. They seem totally oblivious to all around them, including each other. They explore with their noses, poking everywhere, digging under shrubs, rooting in grass, or taking off on tangents to explore inviting slopes. If the ground is wet and the meadow lush, they may paw up and overturn chunks of sod to extricate roots and tubers beneath. The torn-up meadows sometimes look as though an army of boys had dug for earthworms.

The offspring, usually twins, are born in winter in the den and are so tiny and helpless that they would seem to require a dozen years at least to grow to full size. It doesn't take long, however, for nature to fill them with strength and spirit; yearlings are able to handle themselves very capably indeed, and in two or three summers they leave the company of their mother and are on their own.

Even as cubs they exhibit the deceptive awkwardness that characterizes their movements. When on all fours and hunting, the animal swings its hips in a side-to-side motion that seems to lack any grace. When a bear stands up, which is primarily for the purpose of getting a better view of something that has attracted its insatiable curiosity, it looks like a massive hulk of uncoordinated fat and fur.

For the young, the period with their mother is one of profound protection, as humans in Yellowstone and elsewhere have occasionally discovered, for there is no more certain way to place oneself in danger than to get between or even near a grizzly bear mother and

Large ungulates, such as elk, utilize the vegetation heavily, but only
selectively and at certain times of year.

her cub. Around her lies an informal zone of no approach—biologists call it an "individual distance"—a no man's land with a radius of 100 or even 200 yards. The mother is so protective that she reacts almost reflexively to any potentially threatening organism that enters this zone. The two most dangerous animals in her life are men and grizzly boars, so the sow pays attention when they get near. The few assaults on persons hiking in back-country areas of Glacier and Yellowstone national parks have been by mature females with cubs. The first recorded attack by a grizzly in Yellowstone National Park took place in 1907 when a visitor unaware of the danger chased a cub up a tree.

Any person heading into the Yellowstone back country must weigh the very remote possibility of attack against the pleasure to be gained by entering a natural world unregulated by man. "Grizzlies and man can co-exist in the national parks," said Stephen Herrero, a Canadian biologist:

> *However, to accomplish this, people will need to develop a more tolerant and less anthropocentric attitude. Men must go infrequently into the grizzlies' habitat, and then as cautious and alert visitors. Man must temporarily relinquish his role as a tamer, a reducer of wilderness, and enter into an ecosystem in which he may not be the dominant species. This can be the quintessence of man's experience in the national parks, because here man becomes a part of nature. This is the highest purpose our parks can serve.*

Grizzlies happen to require extensive wilderness areas little disturbed by man. Not that they couldn't live in restricted areas; they survive in zoos. But wild grizzlies are not social animals; family groups and individuals have a strong tendency to avoid each other. The result is a natural spacing of bears across the land—one bear for every ten to fifteen square miles of wilderness in Yellowstone.

Many grizzlies used to be spread through brushlands, foothills, and valleys from the Mississippi River to the Pacific Coast and from the Arctic to Mexico. But now in the contiguous United States they have been reduced by human encroachment to enclaves where they are protected. An estimated 37,000 still survive, mostly in Canada and Alaska. But the only major populations of them south of the forty-ninth parallel are in Yellowstone and Glacier national parks, where the wide, wild land they need is still available. Biologists conclude that the final home for these animals will be in national parks and similar reserves.

The Black Bear

Except in spring, visitors seldom see a grizzly, and this is unfortunate. What they more often encounter and, alas, a creature that has made Yellowstone famous, is the black bear panhandling at the roadside. Though it appears to be quite docile and resembles an overgrown dog, the black bear is definitely not man's best friend. A bear that has become addicted to handouts simply regards human beings as walking food conveyors from whom a snack may be gotten by begging, stealing, clawing, biting—or worse.

Black bears, which sometimes have brown or cinnamon-colored fur, weigh up to 500 pounds. Naturally, it takes a great deal of food to satisfy such a hulk. Nature has not only provided for the animal's food requirements quite adequately over the years but has adapted the bear to an environment of mixed forest broken by meadows and open hillsides, where grasses, succulent leafy plants, and woody fruit-bearing shrubs are available. Food from visitors disrupts the natural regime and may harm the bear.

Even worse, cubs become conditioned to the artificial way of life along the roadside and when they have reached adulthood may be addicted to the foods men give them. As summer ends, bears wander along the highway for a while, wondering perhaps where all the cars have gone. They may thus not get themselves sufficiently fattened for winter.

Happily for persons who recognize and appreciate

Overleaf: Cow elk and calf. During the summer months elk are found throughout the park, but in winter most of them migrate to lower elevations.

the value of seeing animals that are truly wild, the panhandling black bear is becoming a thing of the past in Yellowstone. The National Park Service has made a concerted effort to eliminate all unnatural sources of food, both by insisting that human campers leave no scraps of food about to entice the bears, and by strictly enforcing the regulation that prohibits feeding of bears.

A Carefree Life

Apart from roadside feeding spots, most of Yellowstone's wilderness is a place where the wildlife reacts in its own special way to the world about it. We once sat picnicking on the banks of the Firehole River when a mother elk and her calf appeared on the opposite shore, less than fifty yards away. The calf, still with its juvenile spots, was probably two months old. The cow walked regally, diffidently, while the calf kicked up its heels and charged across the meadow. Where Sentinel Creek entered the river, the calf plunged into a shallow pool and bounced up an embankment on the other side, then galloped with total abandon along the edge of the river.

The mother meanwhile reached the creek and, keeping an eye on her calf and an eye on us, stepped through the water and came up on the other bank. The calf saw her, leaped over a fallen log, and sprinted back across the turf, its hoofbeats breaking the silence like the drumming of a grouse. It went so fast that it overshot its mother and dug its hooves into the grass for twenty yards before stopping. By that time it had come to the edge of Sentinel Creek and had almost fallen in. Straightening up, it froze in its tracks at the sight of a flock of young mallards in the water, partly sheltered by a curtain of grass that hung out over the bank. The young elk raised its ears, twisted its head, and pointed its nose at this new phenomenon. The neck went lower and the ears forward, a stance held for at least ten seconds—a long time for a romping elk to be still. Then it looked back toward its mother.

She cocked her ears and surveyed the vicinity, then

Above: Bison eat heartily in summer. *Overleaf*: Winter is a trial for Yellowstone wildlife. Deep snow covers forage, and large animals must struggle through blinding storms.

sank to her knees in the grass and dropped into a position of rest at the river's edge. Her ears relaxed and she commenced to chew her cud. The young elk watched the ducks preen their feathers and drift slowly out into the main stream, then lost interest. Returning to where its mother lay, it bedded down in front of her, almost disappearing from sight in the high growth. The last we saw of them they were still lying there, shaking their ears and getting sleepier and sleepier.

This experience would suggest that the elk are tame; they are not. One cannot walk up to them; they move away when human beings approach too closely. However, they do not seem to be worried by the presence of men. For the elk, man has merely become another animal of the ecosystem, not necessarily compatible but tolerable. The reason for this is simply that this central portion of the park, the Madison and Firehole rivers and Hayden Valley, has been relatively undisturbed for a century. Even though millions of visitors have entered this region, the wildlife and landscape are still very close to their natural state. Visitors came mostly after the national park was established, and then only to observe the animals in their original habitat. The animals have thus had little to fear except their natural predators.

Bison

The elk's close associate on the central plateau, the bison, reacts in the same way. This exclusively American mammal, vastly depleted since the days when millions roamed the continent, had nearly been exterminated by the time Yellowstone became a national park. Indeed, this park was one of the key sanctuaries in which the bison survived as a species. Since the animal is a symbol of something saved, just as the passenger pigeon of the East is a symbol of something lost, we note with a sense of relief that this small portion of original habitat has been successfully preserved.

Yellowstone bison are easily observed in winter, spring, and fall, though sometimes only as black spots on a distant ridge. In summer the herds retreat to high mountain slopes and meadows, far from park roads, but occasional lone bulls do remain in the lower valleys where they can be seen and photographed. The open flats and hills are their accustomed milieu, for their favorite foods—as determined by analyses of stomach contents—are sedges, grasses, and rushes. They may look placid and appear to move slowly, but researchers who try to follow them for a day and note their behavior must often scramble wildly to keep up.

Today the five hundred or so bison in Yellowstone National Park represent one of the few completely wild and free-ranging bison herds in the United States, and the only remnant of the original mountain bison, although they have been hybridized with plains bison stock. They roam at will, migrating in spring and fall and ranging widely in summer. They rarely leave the park. Their environment supplies all they need, but it also presents them with a major problem —getting along in deep snow. Unlike most ungulates they do not paw the snow to get to grasses; rather, they have adapted by swinging their heads from side to side and sweeping the snow away. This behavior allows them to utilize the heavily vegetated, snow-covered bottomlands much of the winter, whereas the elk must occupy slopes that are windblown or relatively free of snow. In times of severest weather the bison may retreat to isolated thermal areas where warmth and fresh green forage can be found even in the harshest winter. Nevertheless, 50 per cent of a given calf crop may perish in the first few years if the weather is severe enough. Swinging the head in heavy snow is a physical strain that takes its toll on smaller animals and any that are weak from other causes. Mortality usually occurs late in winter; hence the calves are lost toward the end of their first year. On rare occasions a group of bison will fall through the ice while crossing a frozen river or lake; thirty-eight died this way in the Yellowstone River in 1946. Bison also are lost occasionally when they fall in hot pools.

Accidents, however, are not a major factor of bison mortality. Neither is brucellosis, sometimes called undulant fever, a disease caused by bacteria that are worldwide in distribution. In Yellowstone it is a natural part of the scene, and the bison seem to suffer no ill effects from it.

Every natural ecosystem has its own controls, however. Without bad weather, accidents, parasites, disease, old age, and other limits to immortality, the populations of these large animals would grow too great for the system to support. They would eat up their food supply and begin to starve, which is in itself an effective natural control.

The Coyote and Its World

Much of the West used to belong more or less to stock growers, who nearly eliminated some of the large predators. Even in Yellowstone National Park it was for a long time federal policy to hunt down coyotes, wolves, and mountain lions. Without these, however, the ecosystem is incomplete and vulnerable to all sorts of alteration. Due to a more enlightened attitude toward predators over the last few decades, some of the original populations are coming back, although slowly. Mountain lions are sighted from time to time, and wolves are returning. Biologists estimate that perhaps a dozen wolves live within and adjacent to the park. Their best hope for survival is to remain there, for state game laws outside still permit the shooting of this rare species. Wolves outside the park may also accidentally become the victims of poisoned bait and cyanide guns intended for coyotes.

Within the park, coyotes have a major role in the economy of nature and are completely protected, as are all native animals. They are by no means rare, and it is now quite clear, from a pioneering study by the eminent naturalist Adolph Murie, that Yellowstone's coyotes fill a gap in the jigsaw puzzle of natural environments. They eat everything from crickets to elk, but their central role is that of a predator upon small rodents. Coyotes subsist mainly on mice and pocket gophers in summer. In winter

they sustain themselves by capturing snowshoe hares and other animals that do not hibernate, or they share with magpies and ravens the cleaning up of carrion. In some years when a large die-off of elk occurs, there are more than enough carcasses for the coyotes.

Deer fawns are a part of the diet, too, and for many years it was thought that coyotes killed so many deer as to endanger their existence. Part of the reason for Murie's researches in the 1930's, which resulted in his *Ecology of the Coyote in the Yellowstone*, was to evaluate this myth. Wild populations of deer and other animals, he reported, were heir to many ailments, among them malnutrition, parasites, disease, debility, and crippling. Murie discovered that when coyotes ate deer it was mostly those that had died from other causes. Only rarely did coyotes pursue and down a fawn, and even then the fawn was weak and probably doomed to die anyway. The coyote was simply culling, a process not detrimental to any species. Murie found no evidence that coyotes endangered healthy adults; sometimes it was the other way around—deer often chased coyotes. He could only conclude, therefore, that the status of deer depended much more on their ability to find suitable food, particularly sagebrush and young Douglas fir, and on how many other deer and how many elk competed for the same food.

The coyote, thus absolved, ceased to be persecuted within the park, and today it is free to fulfill its functions of keeping the weakest individuals of other species from perpetuating their kind and keeping the dead from befouling the environment.

It is easy to overemphasize the carnivores of Yellowstone because they capture our attention and imagination so readily and are so exciting to see in the wild. Far more widespread, however, and far more fundamental to the total economy of Yellowstone's natural world are the vegetarians, most of which one never sees. Altogether they occupy nearly every natural niche in which there is growth, not only on the summits, where those diminutive members of the rabbit family, the pikas, gather herbs, but among the cliffs

Overleaf: Bighorn sheep roam the snow-covered ridges, scratching at patches of withered grass.

and crags, where bighorn sheep subsist on tender grass in summer and woody shrubs in winter. Marmots and wood rats take over piles of rock; muskrats and beaver command the mountain marshes; moose occupy the sedge and willow wetlands and occasionally drier hillsides; tree squirrels make their homes in the upper levels of the forest, whereas ground squirrels prefer more rocky and open terrain; gophers, mice, and rabbits, the staple in many a predator's diet, tunnel the subsoil with their holes or passageways and come out among the thick, concealing grasses of the meadows.

Reptiles and amphibians are also well represented in Yellowstone, though not by many species; there is one species of salamander and one of lizard. Toads and frogs are found at nearly all elevations, and several species of snakes as well as numerous invertebrates live in the park.

The Trumpeter Swan

Having maximum mobility, birds occupy nearly every habitat. One species in particular has a special place in Yellowstone and is a living tribute to the national park idea. The trumpeter swan, largest of North American waterfowl, prefers more marshes than are available in Yellowstone but finds so safe a sanctuary here that it is a regular resident, by the pair on many of the lakes in summer, and by the flock in winter. The park, together with the nearby Red Rock Lakes National Wildlife Refuge, is credited with helping to save the bird from extinction. The population of the species, once down to about seventy individuals, has climbed back into the thousands, thanks to laws affording them protection throughout their range but especially to the preservation of native habitat in the Yellowstone region.

Trumpeter swans need only a few patches of bulrush, sedge, or cattail in which to nest, and the parents and their cygnets can be easily observed in summer, provided visitors do not approach them. Not only swans but a whole congregation of other aquatic creatures can be seen: redwings, goldeneye

If the grass they prefer is covered, elk will resort to bark and conifer
needles to avoid starvation.

ducks, teals, kingfishers, geese, coots, muskrats, and other wetland species. Trumpeters also live in the mountains during winter, frequenting ice-free waters that they share with mallards, geese, and goldeneyes. During a recent midwinter ski patrol, rangers counted seventy-two swans grouped along the ice-free outlet from Yellowstone Lake. Some slept; some drifted; some grazed on grasses along the bank in subzero cold. When they took flight it was with a symphony of trumpeting voices and flapping wings.

Yellowstone has another symbol, the bald eagle— a scavenger but nonetheless a commanding bird. Its elegant, soaring flights above cliffs or over streams and its regal perch on a limb overlooking the wild waters makes it worthy of tribute. Civilization has pushed it into such wilderness regions as this, where it does not face the danger of pesticides applied by man to his environment. The bald eagle, together with other large birds—ospreys, great blue herons, and pelicans—search the waters for fish. The golden eagle and a dozen species of hawks take great numbers of smaller animals, serving in their way to modify the mammal populations and thus influence the ecosystem directly and indirectly.

A Gathering of Elk

In nature a single native ungulate often plays a dominant role in the ecology of specific regions. In the coastal hills and Sierra Nevada of California, it is the mule deer; throughout much of the East, the white tail deer; and during bygone days on the midwest plains, the bison. In the Yellowstone region, probably for the past 10,000 years or more, elk have occupied this key role. Today as many as 15,000 of these members of the deer family inhabit the park during summer. Without a doubt, the total tonnage of such an animal population exceeds that of all other Yellowstone ungulates combined: bison, mule deer, bighorn, moose, and pronghorn. The elk thus have a significant influence on the lives of other creatures within the ecosystem. On one hand, they consume enormous amounts of vegetation and thus affect the development and condition of plant life; on the other, they are themselves important food for a variety of predators and scavengers.

What enables the elk to occupy such a dominant position is not entirely understood, but undoubtedly the wide assortment of food they can thrive on has a great deal to do with it. They are strictly vegetarian, and there are very few plants they reject entirely. During the year their diet may include all kinds of grasses, sedges, and rushes, both green and cured; they subsist on leafy plants of forest and meadow, such as horsetail, pussytoes, lupine, huckleberry, and aster. They browse on wild rose, willow, sage, and other common shrubs. During fall and winter they supplement their diet with conifer needles as well as the bark of aspen and other deciduous trees. A typical year-round diet would be half grass, a quarter browse, and a quarter leafy forbs.

Obviously, this range of acceptable food permits the elk to subsist in several environments, a capacity especially important during the critical winter period. They can adapt to deep snow in the forested Madison-Firehole river drainages, to windswept highlands on Quadrant Mountain, or to open grassland in the lower Yellowstone Valley, where snow is less deep.

Of the four main elk herds in Yellowstone in summer, one is resident all year in the general area of the Firehole, Madison, and Gibbon rivers. Winter is rigorous and the snow heavy in this region, but extensive areas of thermal warmth tide the animals over when environmental stress becomes extreme. The others move. A southern herd of about 4,000 elk descends from its summer home in the southern part of the park down into Grand Teton National Park and the Jackson Hole country. This may not seem practical inasmuch as cold air often settles in Jackson Hole and produces some of the lowest recorded temperatures in the contiguous United States, i.e., down to 60° below zero. But the wind there is less forceful and the snow less deep than in the Yellowstone uplands, and since the migration has gone on for so many years there must be some survival value to it.

Top: Black bear cubs are usually born in the midst of winter and by spring are ready for the season of foraging. *Middle*: Mule deer fawns are born in June, following migration of the deer to their higher spring range. *Bottom*: Mountain lion kitten. The comeback of predators encourages hope that Yellowstone's original balance of animal life can be restored.

In the northwest corner of Yellowstone a herd of approximately 1,500 elk spends the summer in meadows and valleys of the Gallatin Mountains, then migrates to winter ranges in Montana, mostly outside the park. The fourth group, the northern herd, is the largest. It fluctuates between 7,000 and 12,000 animals, and all, or nearly all, migrate, but not as a group. Some do not go very far; they spend the winter, however severe, at lower elevations along the Lamar and Yellowstone river drainages, the largest intact elk winter range remaining in North America, some 200,000 acres. These are the elk that provide the tremendous wildlife display seen from the road between Gardiner and Soda Butte each winter. The rest proceed downstream and spread out along or beyond the northern boundary of the park.

The four herds are not distinct in summer; there is a good deal of intermingling. A few elk scatter in groups along river bottoms and lowland meadows. Gibbon Meadow, Elk Park, and the Lamar and Hayden valleys almost always have a few that can be seen from the Grand Loop drive either early or late in the day. But most climb to high alpine meadows far from any road.

Summer is a time of abundant food for the elk, as for nearly all other creatures in this climate, but Yellowstone summers are short, and the elk must put on many pounds of flesh, a fat energy reserve that will be needed for survival six months hence. Bull elk have an extra requirement: some of their energy goes into the production of antlers, which by fall will be large racks of bone weighing up to twenty pounds.

In September, high-pitched trumpetlike sounds echo across the valleys from ridge to ridge, a piercing sound unlike any other. The bugling of the bull elk means the start of the rutting season, which will last a good six weeks. It is a time of countless sparring matches from which the dominant males emerge to rule over harems of six or so cow elk. By the time of the last bugle call, deep snow has usually fallen, especially at high elevations, and the elk move down from their summer homes and autumn haunts. How-

ever, the first big snowfall of the season does not send wildlife scuttling en masse from the mountains; their movements are gradual. Elk travel easily in snow up to two feet deep, and at the beginning of winter the snows are usually light and powdery and not confining.

A few elk migrate beyond the park as far as sixty miles. Others assemble on traditional winter range at lower elevations. It is then that their winter trials begin, as has happened for thousands of years. Day after day the snows grow deeper, and the elk paw trenches to get at the grasses and sedges beneath. Some may have to trudge for miles through deep snow in order to arrive at traditional winter foraging grounds. One herd of about a hundred elk winters at 9,500 feet elevation on Quadrant Mountain in the Gallatin Range. This is not prime wintering range for elk; it is beset by fierce storms and severe ground blizzards. But the elk go there for one reason: availability of forage. There the wind has blown free much of the snow and they find enough food to compensate for the rigors of the environment. Sometimes they do have to leave when a brief warm period turns a small fall of snow into a crust of ice. Then they move down the mountain to south-facing, windblown ridges sometimes as much as 2,000 feet lower, where forage is more readily available. They may stay there until spring, but they have been known to migrate back to the summit of Quadrant Mountain in the middle of winter.

Good foraging usually continues until January, after which the elk must search with diligence to find enough to eat. Sometimes the snow becomes too deep, too compacted, and too crusted over for the elk to maneuver easily. They then must feed on the sunnier south-facing slopes of the Lamar River Valley or along the Yellowstone River. In such exposed places the weather is likely to be miserable, but what counts is the availability of forage. When they shift to these prime sites they may concentrate for short periods in densities as high as one elk on every two acres. But some will not survive. In heavy winters many will not. This is especially true when populations have reached an upper limit and there is not enough food for all. Winter's severity provides the mechanism that regulates the numbers of Yellowstone ungulates. Contrary to earlier belief, fluctuations in population are normal and necessary to sustain a balanced ecosystem.

It might seem logical that the bulls, healthy and vigorous masters of the rutting season, would be well equipped to survive the winter. On the contrary, they are the most vulnerable. They have expended energy in producing and carrying antlers, which have no survival value after rutting, and during the fall, when other members of the herd were fattening themselves for winter, the bulls ate almost nothing; their interests were more oriented toward mating than survival. Breeding activities are so energetic that the most active bulls lose up to 25 per cent of their weight. They are thus likely to be the first to succumb, even during a mild winter, yet they are probably the most expendable from the standpoint of the overall health of the herd; they have served their purpose and next year younger bulls will assume the reproductive duties.

It is incorrect to think of natural elk mortality as a wasteful whim of nature; rather, fallen elk are vital food for some of Yellowstone's most important animals, the predators and scavengers. Coyotes may rush to the scene, only to find that a cougar or a wolf pack or, if in spring and summer, a grizzly or black bear has arrived there first. Numerous smaller carnivores, such as wolverine, lynx, and red fox, depend upon flesh for their existence; they normally prey on lesser beasts but never pass up a meal of meat, even if a day or two old. The carcass of an elk is usually reduced to scattered skeletal remains and strips of hide within forty-eight hours.

Birds, too, may benefit; ravens, magpies, and bald and golden eagles partake of the scattered feasts. And in the end it is rodents and insects that clean up the remaining scraps. Indeed, the procedure is quite ingenious and indicative of the healthy functioning of the ecosystem. All this is part of the grand scheme of Yellowstone's animals in relation to their environment, where the elk is the most important animal in the middle tier of the pyramid of life.

The Other Ungulates

In considering the number of creatures that feed on much the same plant food as elk—the bison, moose, pronghorn, mule deer, and bighorn—there arises the question of competition, and the fear that one or more of these other animals will be eliminated from the Yellowstone scene. It is true that there is a good deal of overlap in the diets of the park's six ungulates, yet each has evolved specific habits and characteristics that permit it to fill a natural niche and survive. Moose have a digestive system that enables them to subsist on an almost steady diet of evergreen vegetation in winter; their comically long legs adapt them perfectly to negotiate the deepest forest snowpack. Mule deer, and especially the delicate pronghorn, prefer no snow at all; both seek the lower elevations in winter, usually on the sage- and grass-covered flats just west and south of Gardiner. Bighorn often feed alongside elk in summer and winter, but their nimbleness in negotiating rocky cliffs gives them access to forage that no other species can reach. And the bison swinging their ponderous heads can sweep away snow and succeed in greater depths of snow than can elk.

Yellowstone today has many meanings to many people. But perhaps the value that transcends all others in a world of shrinking natural environments is the wealth of native life supported by this wild land. In the final analysis we stand in awe before one striking fact: except for primitive man himself, every species of animal known to be in Yellowstone when white man first entered and described the place is living there today.

The Explorers

8

Neither geysers nor wilderness nor solitude nor the full moon over Mount Sheridan have attracted men to Yellowstone as much as have wild animals—and this has been true during the 11,000 years of man's occupation of this region. Ice Age mammals such as mammoths and ancestors of the modern bison first drew prehistoric hunters into what was doubtless a bleak, rugged, bouldery land more hostile than it is now. We can only guess what was in the minds of those earliest people, but it seems safe to conjecture that they did not come merely to observe wild animal herds in the valleys or the habits of mountain species. They came for food.

Evidence of early hunters in the valley of the Yellowstone River, largely below what is now the park, has been found in two principal forms: projectile points very likely used to bring down bison, deer, and elk, and fire pits in which to roast the meat. It is apparent that from the beginning animals were distinctly outmaneuvered by human intellect; there is evidence of communal hunting by small groups of men who drove animals up to blinds where other men lay ready to slay them with bows and arrows.

These earliest people must have seen the numerous thermal springs and geysers, but they left no record of it. We have only scant evidence that they ever held the region in any kind of superstitious awe. According to one report, later Indians avoided the thermal areas because they heard loud noises like thunder and their children couldn't sleep. Moreover, the earth trembled, and it was thus clear to them that spirits living there did not want men around. Nevertheless, the lure of animals was so great, for hunters at least, that the thermal features were generally bypassed with probably not much more attention than was needed to avoid their dangers.

The only primitive peoples known to have lived year round in what is now Yellowstone National Park were Sheepeaters, mountain dwellers of Shoshone and Bannock Indian origins, whose existence depended upon hunting bighorn sheep. The first European explorers found them dressed in sheepskins and

The Hayden Expedition, 1871. The leader, Ferdinand V. Hayden, is seated in rear center; the famous photographer William H. Jackson stands at far right.

said that they were a simple, peaceful people less advanced than their neighbors. Sheepeaters used horns and antlers in fashioning bows, sinews of deer and elk in making strings, and quills of porcupine for ornamentation. In exchange for exotic objects brought in by explorers, they offered animal skins.

Trappers and Traders

Skins were exactly what the explorers wanted. The first adventurous pioneers from the eastern edge of the continent were trappers, bent on enriching themselves with the bounty of the land, especially the pelts of fur-bearing mammals. For many years, of course, there were fewer hunters than wild animals and it would have been hard for an individual trapper to imagine how the great abundance of game could ever be diminished. Yet the ecosystems were as fragile then as now, and disturbances that seemed unimportant to individual hunters added up to a major threat as more and more hunters and trappers poured into the West.

Up to that time there had never been enough Indian hunting to cause a serious depletion of animal numbers either in the mountains or on the plains. Now the Indians were threatened not only by an invasion of their lands but by competition for the wildlife on which they depended. Clashes occurred between Indians and newcomers in the Yellowstone region. The Sheepeaters remained essentially peaceful, but Crows and Piegans routed as many of the invaders as possible, and since some of the incoming aliens could read and write, there are recorded descriptions of hair-raising episodes in the pursuit of pelts.

It is hard to say when wandering trappers first climbed into the upper reaches of the Yellowstone River, although there are hints that some did so around the beginning of the nineteenth century. The first of whom any reliable record remains was John Colter, a Virginian who became something of a Daniel Boone of the Rocky Mountains. He spent nearly three years with the Lewis and Clark expedition and remained in the West as a trapper. Evidence

indicates that he entered the Yellowstone region in 1807. His purpose was more calculating than just to take furs for himself; he advised the Indians that trading posts were being set up where pelts could be exchanged for trinkets, guns, and whiskey. It is easy to see what pressures this placed on Yellowstone's fur-bearing animals.

In the late 1820's a party of trappers was attacked by Indians, and one of the intruders, a nineteen-year-old tenderfoot named Joe Meek, was separated from his companions and compelled to wander for days in the bitterest cold of winter. He managed to survive the ordeal and in due course came to a basin of hot springs and geysers where, with great relief, he rejoined his friends. Compared with the snow and icy nights he had just been through, the steam and boiling water were a godsend. "If this is Hell," he is quoted as saying, "it's a heap better climate than the one I just left."

Traffic of trappers into the Yellowstone increased and only the harassment and delay caused by the Indians prevented far more pelts from being gathered. When American and Canadian fur companies entered the region in full force, trapping became so well organized that trappers penetrated even the most remote places.

Although the fur trade diminished after 1840, owing to decreasing markets and a decline in populations of certain fur-bearing species, the influx of guides, scouts, prospectors, miners, wagoneers, emigrants, horse thieves, fishermen, hunters, ranchers, priests, engineers, and naturalists continued. And why not? This was obviously free and open land, or would be after the Indian threat was eliminated. And if there was anything the frontiersman demanded, anything that was the very essence of what he came after, it was the freedom to live exactly where he wanted and do exactly as he pleased. Here, the land was his who could plow it and make a living from it. The trees were his to cut, the birds his to bring down out of the sky, and the fish his to take up out of the streams. Fur-bearing mammals belonged to whoever

Top: *The Hayden Expedition crossing the Mirror Plateau, 1871.* Bottom: *A scene at camp during the Hayden Expedition.*

could trap them or get them within rifle range. Indeed, the more mammals or birds he could shoot in one day, the greater his prowess and the more enduring his fame. At the height of the slaughter on the plains, the best buffalo hunters shot 250 bison a day.

An overpowering tradition grew out of these conditions and before long men came to believe that since they had always gone into these mountains and taken away the game, they thus always could and would; it was their God-given right and no one was going to stop them. This could hardly be disputed; they found in the Bible itself authority for man's conquest over nature. And God helped those who helped themselves.

The Coming of the Curious

From the view of man as a competitive biological species, these settlers were simply asserting their territorial rights, though not without conflict. Although the Yellowstone region at one time or another was claimed by England, France, Spain, and the United States, in no case was it ever purchased from its original owners, the Indians, or even transferred by treaty, except for the purchase of a small piece of land from the Crow Indians. Such negligence, though it still persists, would be widely condemned today, but in the nineteenth century Indians were regarded as renegades who had to be removed, or as obstructionists who were not making full use of the country and should give way to men who could utilize it more productively. Even after the young United States took formal claim to the land, Yellowstone belonged successively to Louisiana, Missouri, Oregon, Washington, Nebraska, Dakota, and, ultimately, to Montana, Idaho, and Wyoming.

Despite all this territorial manipulation and the increasing numbers of hunters and trappers who crisscrossed the Yellowstone plateaus, great herds of animals still remained in the high country. While bison were being slaughtered on the plains below, thousands quietly grazed on the upper reaches of the Madison and Yellowstone river drainages. One journal after another, however, described incidents in which wild animals, especially bears, were shot and killed. One party proudly spoke of killing a family of grizzly bears and a boar that weighed 960 pounds.

There seemed to be nothing wrong with this, for in the history of human conscience few voices had opposed the conquest of animal life. On the contrary, man had evolved as a hunter, and evolutionary changes come very slowly. Not in a century, or even a millennium, would his habits be easily altered.

Men had been intelligent enough to ally themselves with dogs and horses to add hunting skills that men themselves lacked: high speed and a keen sense of smell. Assyrian kings with arrows, bows, and spears had no greater desire than to be remembered as "mighty hunters before the Lord." Inca kings reserved the hunting of vicuñas to themselves. Over a span of four centuries, hundreds of thousands of animals were publicly slain in Rome; under Trajan, for example, 11,000 were killed in 123 days. Marco Polo described the killing of thousands of bears, stags, roebucks, and other beasts in China, and said, "It is an admirable sight, when the lion is let loose in pursuit of the animal, to observe the savage eagerness and speed with which he overtakes it."

Nothing turned all this into a systematic slaughter like the invention of firearms and the refinement of traps—in other words, the coming of technology. Man the hunter was no longer also hunted, as he had been in primitive days; he became a much more effective hunter himself. In addition, it has been a peculiar and almost universal tenet in the American West that the greater the hunter, the greater the man.

Clearly, then, nearly every human mind accepted the notion that wilderness ought to be conquered and "put to good use." While 90 per cent of Ohio was originally covered with forests, an era of cutting and clearing reduced that cover to 15 per cent. So the precedent and practice were clear, and the word "restraint" was in hardly anyone's vocabulary.

Fortunately, Yellowstone escaped much of the rape of the land and its wildlife that elsewhere accom-

Top: *The Hayden Expedition camps at Yellowstone Lake, 1871.* Middle: *William H. Jackson, the first official photographer of Yellowstone.* Bottom: *Hunters with meat for the Hayden Expedition, 1871.*

Yellowstone in the 1870's. Top: *Mammoth Hot Springs.* Bottom: *Lone Star Geyser.*

panied man's westward movement across the nation. More than anything else, the reason for this was Yellowstone's inaccessibility. While a considerable number of explorers did get to it, many others attempted and failed. Men no doubt dreamed of utilizing its treasures of forest and wildlife, but distances were much too great. Shipping logs to market was more expensive than shipping furs, and the fur trade itself had already diminished. Moreover, the nearest railroad was 400 miles away in Utah, and even that was not built before 1869. Indians had grown more hostile with the increasing encroachment and faithless acts of the invaders. Thus a considerable supply of food, energy, nerve, and perseverance was required to get to Yellowstone, and some of the explorers must have felt as though they were embarking on suicide missions.

Then in 1834 a subtle change occurred. Warren Ferris, a surveyor and employee of the American Fur Company, came to the region because he was curious rather than commercial. He had heard the tales and legends of spouting springs and wanted to see them. He was, in effect, the first tourist to arrive in Yellowstone and the first to describe the geysers. To be sure, stories of the thermal features had been exchanged around campfires, and Yellowstone's wonders had been extolled by such fur traders as John Colter and Jim Bridger. But the mountain men had reputations for stretching the truth, and their tales of Yellowstone were seldom taken seriously. Yet the exaggerated reports describing great glass mountains (Obsidian Cliff), petrified animals in petrified hills (Specimen Ridge), and the geyser basins were a powerful lure.

When reliable observers such as Ferris began to say that the strange reports were true, a few men began entering the Yellowstone country more out of curiosity than for hunting. Even among trappers there were some who became enchanted with values other than furs. Osborne Russell, a twenty-year-old Maine farm boy who had turned to the business of trading and trapping, led a hunt into the region in 1835 and was so impressed with the Lamar River

Valley that he almost wished he could spend the rest of his life there. He called it Secluded Valley and wrote in his journal that "happiness and contentment seemed to reign in wild romantic splendor surrounded by majestic battlements."

Considering all the traffic into and out of the Upper Yellowstone River Valley between 1807 and 1870, it surprises us that the American public still had only a hazy notion of what was there. But no rapid communications other than telegraph existed in those days; no reflex cameras were available to capture the geysers on film, and, indeed, no tangible proof whatever existed to supplement the patently unbelievable descriptions.

The Cook–Folsom–Peterson Expedition

This era of mystery ended with the accomplishments of three successive expeditions in the summers of 1869, 1870, and 1871. All three climbed up into the Yellowstone country with more or less similar goals: to prove the truth or falsity of the rumors.

The first to go were Charles Cook, David Folsom, and William Peterson, all of whom had spent enough time in mining camps or on woodland trails to be well versed in survival techniques. They moved up the Yellowstone River in chilly September, to the accompaniment, they said, of howling wolves, roaring mountain lions, and bugling elk. Snow caught them, but their first look into the Grand Canyon of the Yellowstone River justified all the struggle. They explored the falls, the mud volcano area upstream, then Yellowstone Lake, Shoshone Lake, and the geyser basins.

Almost never before, as far as the record goes, had men so interested in Yellowstone because of its joy and beauty come to see it. They were virtually stunned by the tremendous collection and variation of natural phenomena. In describing their first view of Great Fountain Geyser, Cook wrote: "The setting sun shining into the spray and steam drifting towards the mountains, gave it the appearance of burnished gold, a wonderful sight. We could not contain our enthusiasm; with one accord we all took off our hats and yelled with all our might."

On returning to Helena, Montana Territory, they were a little apprehensive about describing their adventures to the town's important businessmen, for fear of being disbelieved. Nevertheless their stories had an immediate impact (a descriptive text was later published) and convinced the surveyor-general of the territory, Henry D. Washburn, and others that perhaps old Jim Bridger had been right after all and there was indeed something worth examining along the headwaters of the Yellowstone and Madison Rivers.

No one knows exactly where or how, but the idea of preserving the Yellowstone wilderness and preventing its being settled or subdivided began to be heard. Cook said that he and his partners discussed the matter in camp near the Firehole River and deplored the prospect of settlers taking up the land for private use. They wanted as many people as possible to see what they had seen and be able to travel through the wilds as freely. None had a notion of what should be done, but they had a vague feeling that the government should not allow the region to be despoiled. Their inability to focus on a course of action is perfectly understandable in light of the fact that few precedents had been set for the establishment of large public parks.

There had been game laws, of course. Otto the Great (912–973), first Emperor of the Holy Roman Empire, proclaimed the first closed season on elk. But the setting aside of a specific parcel of real estate for preservation of wildlife seems to have happened only for the benefit of royalty. It is possible that the ancient Sumerians or Babylonians or Egyptians did this. Justinian, the Roman lawgiver, is said to have laid down the principle that beaches and shorelines belonged to all the people, but that was an exception to the rule. The Chinese created parks for displaying animals, and in India, well before the time of Christ, there were protected places "where beasts could roam about without any fear of man." Germanic princes proclaimed that certain lands belonging to the tribe as a whole were to be reserved for hunting by princes only. England's Richard the Lionhearted had seven villages removed in order to make a fenced-in game park for his use. Even though the public was excluded, these were at least preserves—of a sort.

And so developed the concepts of park, game park, deer park, city park—lands under central control. But what of a whole landscape for all the people? Royal preserves were at times thrown open—or usurped—and the public went in to hunt when kings were deposed. But in the newly formed democracies, private preserves supported by the public treasury were anathema, and in the United States a new conscience of conservation had begun to evolve.

Cook, Folsom, and Peterson may have been unaware of it, but in 1832 Congress had established the Hot Springs Reservation in Arkansas Territory. By that act four square miles of land were set aside to preserve outstanding hot springs even then being utilized for bathing purposes. The idea behind this reservation was that of a "spa" to be used for medicinal purposes. There was neither management nor development of the area until after the turn of the century. Cook and his colleagues are more likely to have known that five years prior to their expedition President Abraham Lincoln had signed an act of Congress granting the Yosemite Valley to the state of California for purposes of public use and recreation.

The Washburn Expedition

The same kind of action was obviously brewing for Yellowstone. Henry Washburn was a young lawyer still in his thirties, a slender, six-foot, blue-eyed blond who had fought in the Civil War, become a Union major-general, and been elected for two terms as an Indiana congressman. Now he had come west under appointment by President Ulysses S. Grant as surveyor-general of Montana Territory. Nor was he the only eminent Montanan interested in Yellowstone. If all the rumors were true, if Cook and Folsom were correct, if the reported wonders could become great tourist attractions—then the railroads would be among the first to benefit. No one was more aware of this than Nathaniel P. Langford, an advocate of the Northern Pacific Railway. Langford, who was the same age as Washburn, was a banker and former collector of internal revenue for Montana Territory. He was also an accomplished organizer, and historians now regard him as the driving force behind the Washburn expedition of 1870.

But Washburn was still the leader and probably the only available man who could have led so many men who were themselves intelligent, accomplished, and determined: Samuel T. Hauser, president of a Helena bank; Warren Gillette, a merchant; Truman C. Everts, former territorial assessor of internal revenue, and his assistant, Walter Trumbull; Cornelius Hedges, a lawyer and correspondent; and Jacob Smith, a former Helena businessman. There were nineteen men in all, counting cooks and packers and the military escort, under Second Lieutenant Gustavus C. Doane.

Owing to continued Indian hostility, they entered the mountains in an uneasy state of mind, and a few may have resigned themselves to the assumption that some would not come back alive. On August 22, 1870, they departed from Fort Ellis, near Bozeman, Montana, and headed south, following the Cook and Folsom route into the valley of the Upper Yellowstone River.

Troubles plagued them—lost men, horses, and trails; bad weather; illness; difficult terrain; mud; accidents; disputes; confusion; and homesickness—but they also made a great deal of progress. They named and measured Tower Falls. Washburn climbed the prominent mountain south of there and returned with such enthusiasm for all he saw that the group named the peak after him.

They continued upstream, measuring, identifying, describing, naming—the most scientific group yet to visit the Yellowstone region. They clambered over cliffs, descended into canyons, peered into the throats of boiling cauldrons, and climbed mountain peaks.

All doubtless kept on the alert for Indians (to whom their horses and guns would have been great prizes) and, in a wilderness so perilous, tried to see to it that no one got lost.

In this last they failed. While exploring on the south side of Yellowstone Lake, Everts became separated from the party, and on the following day, when his horse took fright and ran away, he was also separated from his matches, gun, blankets, and fishing tackle—a major disaster on the frontier. And especially so during the unpredictable chilly weather of Yellowstone in September. "Mr. Everts must have been entirely unaccustomed to a wild life," wrote the Earl of Dunraven in *The Great Divide* some years later, "else he never would have lost his horse, left his rifle on the saddle when he dismounted, or gone about without a supply of matches in his pocket."

What happened to Everts during the next thirty-five days is unparalleled in Yellowstone history. The Earl of Dunraven continued:

> *This unfortunate gentleman wandered alone, through woods and over mountains, totally unarmed, and with no other instruments or appliances than two knives and a pair of small field-glasses. Strange to say, he allowed himself almost to perish daily, for want of fire, for nearly a fortnight, before he thought of kindling one by means of the lenses of his glasses. One of the fearfully cold storms which suddenly arise in these latitudes came on, and he would have succumbed to cold and exposure had he not managed to reach a group of hot springs. As it was, he was severely frosted on both feet. In that neighbourhood he remained seven days, keeping himself warm by lying on the hot incrustation surrounding a little boiling spring, in which he cooked an insignificant supply of roots.*
>
> *The day before his rescue he lost his glasses also; an additional misfortune which nearly overthrew the slight remnant of life and reason which still held out against the fatal effects of his pro-*

*longed and unparalleled sufferings. At an earlier
stage of his adventures he had even lost his knives.
In fact, after commencing with his horse, he lost
everything of use that he had with him; and the
only marvel is that he did not lose his head also,
and his life.*

Everts subsisted for more than a month on little
else than thistles, roots, and grass. "Everything that
could happen to him did occur," wrote the Earl.
"His feet were badly frozen; he lost all he had originally, and everything that he made; he even got rid
of one of his shoes; he slipped into some boiling water
and scalded his hip severely; and it was apparently
his nightly custom to tumble into the fire and burn
himself."

But the Earl allowed that "the captious critic of
his [Everts's] actions would starve as soon as anybody
else," and it does indeed attest to his perseverance
that he survived so long with so little. Not until the
Washburn party had returned to Helena was he
rescued, and then by two other men who came into
the mountains specifically to search for him. At that
time his weight had fallen to fifty pounds. So ema-
ciated, incoherent, crippled, and near death was he
that not for weeks could he walk again. Ultimately
he recovered fully.

The rest of the original Washburn party was delayed by about seven days searching for Everts. They
barely missed him once, but eventually had to give
him up for lost and go on because their own supply
of food was getting low.

Crossing the Continental Divide they entered the
Upper Geyser Basin just as a giant geyser erupted. It
was a welcome relief from their recent troubles, and
a breathtaking introduction to the major thermal
features of the Firehole River. They camped not far
from a geyser which, in due course, Washburn named
"Old Faithful." They went on giving other principal
geysers names that still endure—Beehive, Castle,
Grotto, Giant, and Giantess—before they must have
collapsed with exhaustion at sundown.

There was little time to stay in this "most remarkable valley," as Washburn called it. On September 19
they moved down the Firehole, past more geysers and
springs than they could possibly measure or study in
years, let alone days, and camped where the Gibbon
and Firehole rivers join to become the Madison.

No doubt their minds were spinning with the great
assemblage of sights they had seen and sounds they
had heard, and if there were ever a time to suggest
that parts of this land be reserved for public enjoyment, it was now. Langford claims that that is exactly
what took place, and he attributes to Hedges the
thought "that there ought to be no private owner-
ship of any portion of that region, but the whole
ought to be set apart as a great National Park, and
that each one of us ought to make an effort to have
this accomplished."

Although such a conversation was not mentioned
in any of the diaries of the other participants, Hedges
confirms it in a note added to the publication of his
diary by the Montana Historical Society in 1904. He
says: "It was at the first camp after leaving the
Lower Geyser Basin when all were speculating which
point in the region we had been through would
become most notable, when I first suggested uniting
all our efforts to get it made a national park, little
dreaming such a thing were possible."

In any case, this was an idea whose time had come,
not by lightning revelation beside a stream but as
another significant step in the switch from conquest
to conservation of nature, a momentous change in
thinking that had had to germinate for centuries
before it could be widely accepted. Herodotus, the
Greek historian, said that the ancient Persians had a
reverence for rivers and never polluted them. Plato
deplored the destruction of forests and the ruination
of rivers in the world he knew. Cicero took issue with
the games and spectacles in Roman arenas and asked,
"What possible pleasure can it be to a man of culture
when a puny human being is mangled by a tremen-
dously powerful beast, or a splendid beast transfixed
by a spear?"

Three early views of Yellowstone. Top: Falls on the Gardner River. Middle: Yellowstone River, 1869. Bottom: Tower Creek, as photographed by William H. Jackson on the Hayden Expedition, 1871.

By 1870 the citizens of the United States were tiring of industrial changes that destroyed their favorite landscapes, and they were in the midst of a back-to-nature movement that reflected itself in poetry, art, and community actions. Ecological concepts were beginning to be understood; Thoreau had talked of saving woods and swamps and of having national preserves, and had said that in wildness was the preservation of the world. Emerson's essays are likely also to have had some influence on the more sophisticated explorers in the Yellowstone. And George Catlin, the pioneer artist, had declared as early as 1833 that there ought to be a "nation's park" to preserve both Indians and animals, especially the vanishing bison, in their wild and natural state.

But ideas die unless revived and fought for, and we do know that Hedges urged a united effort to get a park established. He prepared newspaper articles about the expedition and the Yellowstone. So did Washburn. Langford wrote an article for a national magazine, *Scribner's Monthly*, and the following winter went east to the States to deliver a series of lectures before distinguished audiences. One of his listeners, Ferdinand V. Hayden, then head of the Geological Survey of the Territories, was so stimulated by Yellowstone and the tide of interest in it that he petitioned Congress for an appropriation of $40,000 to carry out an official survey of the area.

Hayden had come close to the Yellowstone on previous travels, and so he knew the region to some degree. Congress appropriated the money for his survey, and he had no trouble recruiting men for a stirring, if hazardous, trip to this well-publicized domain. The railroads even shipped his men and supplies without charge; the benefits of future tourism were too great to ignore. The party consisted of twenty men, including artists, scientists, and physi-

Morrison   Witham   Holt   Lieut. Lindsley

Trip to Fall river 1897

Left: *United States Army ski patrol, 1897.* Top: *The pioneer photographer, Frank Jay Haynes, in Norris Geyser Basin, 1887.* Bottom: *A patrol in 1894 investigating elk in deep snow.*

cians. Among those who were to make a lasting visual record of the trip were William H. Jackson, the photographer, and Thomas Moran, then on his way to becoming one of the West's most famous artists. These men would at long last present to the world tangible proof that extraordinary natural wonders did exist in this region.

The Hayden Expedition

The Hayden expedition entered the Yellowstone country in June, 1871, in association with a military reconnaissance mission headed by two engineers, Captains John W. Barlow and David P. Heap. They were there expressly at the direction of the noted General Philip H. Sheridan, who had been very much impressed by Lieutenant Doane's report on the Washburn expedition of the previous year.

It was a summer of successful exploration for both parties. Notebooks and journals were filled with daily records of observations. Measurements, charts, maps, photographs, and sketches were accumulated. Perhaps most significantly, men had begun to appreciate the scenery for its own sake, the quiet joys of wilderness, the intangible values. "The view is wonderfully fine in every direction," Hayden wrote. He spoke of the view from Mount Washburn as one of the finest he had ever seen, and made a not too erroneous assessment of the fundamental geologic values of the region. He also thrilled to the thermal features. "Nothing ever conceived by human art," he wrote, "could equal the peculiar vividness and delicacy of coloring of these remarkable prismatic springs. . . . Life becomes a privilege and a blessing after one has seen and thoroughly felt these incomparable types of nature's cunning skill."

If the landscape Hayden and his comrades examined was to stay more or less the way they saw it, time for action was growing short. Already claims were being staked out around Mammoth Hot Springs and plans were in the offing to establish a bathing resort there. Gold had been discovered just a few miles away. There was nothing to control the hunting of animals or the breaking away of picturesque and delicate rock formations by souvenir-hunters. Sportsmen who had all but eliminated the bison on the plains would now turn to hunting the bison of the mountains, the last great herd of which grazed on the Yellowstone plateaus. Sooner or later sheepherders would comb the mountains looking for places to bring their flocks. On this point, John Muir, then a man in his thirties living in the Yosemite Valley of California, would have had a word: "As sheep advance, flowers, vegetation, grass, soil, plenty, and poetry vanish."

To keep all this from vanishing, a concerted effort to get the park established was launched in the fall of 1871. As we look back on the proceedings of that winter, we are astonished at the rapid progress. But we must remember that Yellowstone was not even a part of the United States. It was a distant entity far out beyond the plains and among the territories that were just being explored. Wyoming, in fact, had been organized as a territory only three years before. Neither it nor Montana would become states of the Union for another two decades. So the establishment of Yellowstone had little immediacy to the rest of the nation; the only way in which it was known at all was through Jackson's photographs and Moran's sketches, an exhibit of which Hayden placed in the rotunda of the United States Capitol as a backdrop for geological specimens from the area.

One can almost say that only a few groups of men knew about Yellowstone—those who fought to protect it, those who opposed it, and those who enacted the law. Identical bills were introduced in both the House and Senate on December 18, 1871. Hayden, Langford, and William H. Clagett, the delegate from Montana Territory, saw to it that every member of Congress was fully informed, not only by receipt of printed material but by personal interview as well.

There was a great deal of support for the proposal. Montanans wanted to follow the Yosemite example, by which Congress would carve the land out of Wyoming Territory and present it to Montana as a grant for a state park. That offered more problems than it solved, however, chiefly because it would have precipitated a battle between Wyoming and Montana, and the park could have been delayed or lost in the process. As it happened, the measure wound up not even specifying that the area become a national park. It was reserved, said the bill, "from settlement, occupancy, or sale under the laws of the United States, and dedicated and set apart as a public park or pleasuring-ground for the benefit and enjoyment of the people." The bill conveyed responsibility to the Secretary of the Interior and instructed him to establish rules and regulations "for the preservation, from injury or spoliation, of all timber, mineral deposits, natural curiosities, or wonders within said park, and their retention in their natural condition."

As a public park established by the federal government, it was, in effect, a national park. The proposal received increasing encouragement from around the country, especially from parts of the railroad industry, which was very influential at that time. On the other hand, many people, lawmakers included, must have considered it piffling legislation, and perhaps this is one reason that it sailed so easily through committees. When it came up for debate the whole project was criticized by a few persons as being unnecessary because men could not do anything to hurt the natural wonders anyway, and unfair because it deprived settlers of so large and choice a section of land.

That was distinctly a minority view, and always has been. A major reason for wanting the park was commercial, of course, with the vast opportunities for tourism. But there seems to be little question that the overwhelming purpose was altruistic: a pride in the country and a desire to preserve its beauties for present and future generations to see and enjoy. A great republic, as the feeling went, should possess a great park. This feeling has been summed up in remarks attributed to Cornelius Hedges: "It seems to me that God made this region for all the people and all the world to see and enjoy forever. It is im-

possible that any individual should think that he can own any of this country for his own in fee. This great wilderness does not belong to us. It belongs to the nation. Let us make a public park of it and set it aside . . . never to be changed but to be kept sacred always."

Attempts were made to recommit the measure and thus delay it, but these were defeated. Congress happened to be in an economy mood so serious that Hayden had to promise a lapse of several years before appropriations would be requested for running the park.

In just a little over two months after its introduction the measure was approved by Congress, and on March 1, 1872, it was signed into law by President Grant. But like other such enterprises that followed in the world's great wilderness areas, it was soon discovered that laws do not establish, protect, or manage anything. Only men do that.

Excelsior Geyser, now dormant, used to erupt to 300 feet in height. Haynes took this photograph of it in 1888, the year it ceased eruption.

9

A New Experiment

The park should so far as possible be spared the vandalism of improvement.

House Report 1076,
Forty-ninth Congress, 1886

"Retention in their natural condition." So said the act of Congress that authorized the setting aside of Yellowstone as a "public park" in March, 1872, but the "wonders and curiosities" of the region were still in jeopardy, law or no law. A large federal park was at that time an incomprehensible oddity to a great many people and a nearly complete reversal of the prevailing attitude toward nature.

Hayden was, of course, elated. "That our legislators," he said, "at a time when public opinion is so strong against appropriating the public domain for any purpose however laudable, should reserve, for the benefit and instruction of the people, a tract of 3,578 square miles, is an act that should cause universal joy throughout the land."

Unfortunately, the act was defective almost to the point of disaster. As a political instrument it left much to be desired. It should by all means have specified the precise kind of administration that would apply to the park, which laws would govern, and what courts would try criminal cases originating within the park. All it said was that the Secretary of the Interior would make regulations. The act provided against "wanton destruction," but did not specify what that meant, or how hunting for food differed from hunting for sport.

The idea of a national park was so new that no one could foresee all the problems that would arise. Had this been only a game refuge, or a group of geysers fenced off for public exhibition, the problem might have been easier, but Congress had something more in mind, although there were no precedents. The idea needed a "push in the right direction," but no one knew which was the right direction. The concept of national parks did not suddenly appear, waiting to be seized and carried forward; it had to be nurtured, tested, revised.

First came official neglect. The act had established Yellowstone as a public park, and Montanans in particular wanted the government to move in and make it immediately and easily accessible. That did not happen, for Hayden had promised that funds would

Gateway arch near Gardiner, Montana, dedicated by President Theodore Roosevelt, April 24, 1903.

not be requested for a while. Nevertheless, visitors flocked to Yellowstone, and since there was virtually no protection, the park remained extremely vulnerable. Some persons thought it was intended to preserve game for hunting—so they came to hunt. Nathaniel Langford was appointed the first superintendent, but there was little he could do without funds or law enforcement officers. A series of park officials followed him, some more attuned to the park idea than others, but all unfortunately victims of a political appointment system that worked consistently to the detriment of the park.

Yellowstone Damaged

Nature's sufferings at the hands of man continued unabated. Grass and forest fires were set accidentally as well as deliberately, and since there was little fire suppression equipment, some fires burned for weeks. Poaching continued. Bison were shot by tourists. "Head-hunting" became a profitable commercial venture because trophy heads of bison could be sold for up to $300 apiece. Hundreds of animals, mostly elk, were slain each year, some for hides, some just for sport. When bears once bothered several workers in the park, men set out to kill off all troublesome bears, and often did so by very cruel means.

Not only animal life suffered. There seemed to be an ineluctable human compulsion to touch, break, and collect natural objects, a tendency as strong in caves and petrified forests as in geyser basins. Scientists, tourists, and other collectors broke off delicate, fragile encrustations from around hot springs and geysers and went away "loaded with specimens." An entire geyser cone was shipped to Washington, D.C., for display at the Smithsonian Institution. Bath houses were built at Mammoth Hot Springs, and bathing places were dug in the limestone.

Visitors threw everything imaginable into the geysers and hot springs—rocks, logs, limbs, coins, bottles, paper—just to see what would happen to such objects or how high they would be hurled in an eruption. In the summer of 1885 a Chinese laundry-man washing clothes in a thermal spring accidentally discovered that soap thrown into a hot pool caused an eruption. On one occasion, a laundry tent set over a spring behind the hotel at Old Faithful was wrecked by an unexpected eruption during working hours. The cause of this phenomenon is that soap reduces the surface tension of the spring, which in turn upsets the delicate balance between hot water and steam. If conditions are right, the disruption of this equilibrium permits subterranean steam to surge upward and eject a column of water.

The soaping process gave men some control over the activity of thermal springs and was seized upon immediately as great fun for tourists. Visitors who had traveled thousands of miles needed no longer wait for a geyser to erupt on its own schedule. Although this tampering with nature did not work every time it was tried, there were remarkable successes on geysers that rarely erupted, and even on hot springs that had not been known to erupt at all. Tourists and guides recklessly attempted to coax hot springs into action by pouring great quantities of soap and concentrated lye into them and in doing so sometimes caused irreparable damage to the spring. "If visitors could have their way," said one observer at the time, "the beautiful blue springs and basins of the geysers would be 'in the suds' constantly throughout the season." Park authorities shortly put a stop to the throwing of any objects into thermal features, though even today it takes a herculean effort and an occasional stiff fine to control these inclinations.

The national park idea, novel as it was, began to exert a strong appeal—but not necessarily as Congress intended. Excursion parties of up to 150 persons and 300 horses came to Yellowstone, stirring up great clouds of dust. Bandits entered and held up stagecoaches. Ranchers brought in their cattle. Squatters moved in, staked claims, and took up residence on the assumption that the national park idea was so absurd that the park would soon be abolished and opened to settlement, and they wanted to be there when this took place. One man opened a saloon.

The early tourist era. Top: *Group on Minerva Terrace, Mammoth Hot Springs, 1888.*
Bottom: *Tourists on Grotto Geyser Cone, 1908.*

Others cut grass and trees, gathered wood, lit forest fires, and helped themselves to the wildlife. Unless some action was taken to protect the animals, a visitor noted, there would be none left to protect. The Indians reacted to the changes brought by increased tourism in Yellowstone, and several bloody skirmishes ensued. Both Bannock and Nez Perce Indians swept through the park, robbing, attacking, injuring, and killing not only members of tourist parties but survey parties and other groups.

The first superintendents could do very little. Not for six years was any money appropriated for the park and then only $10,000 for the first year. Little more than talk was possible—talk with tourists, with settlers, with Indians, soldiers, hunters. And even when funds did become more plentiful, the earliest superintendents found that they had no authority to arrest or punish or even to remove anyone from the park. The Yellowstone Act was simply inadequate and the officers were nearly powerless.

A Time of Trial

Despite these handicaps, some progress was made in constructing accommodations and roads. There was, in fact, almost too much of this kind of progress. Railroad companies desperately fought to build rail lines, not only to the edge of the park (which they did), but into it, through it, among its beauties, and out again. Park personnel, seeing natural pillars of stone that looked as though they were about to fall, trussed them up with wooden supports. They altered the flow of hot spring waters from normal run-off channels. Later there would be proposals to operate an electric railway using current generated at the falls of the Yellowstone River, and to install an elevator to the bottom of the Grand Canyon of the Yellowstone.

The park had its enemies, including men in Congress. Bills were introduced to repeal the Yellowstone Act so that the land could be opened to settlement. The park idea faltered for a time on the brink of collapse. In addition to lack of law enforcement, the system of civil administration in the park deteriorated because of inept management and political chicanery. As a result, the Army was asked to step in and run the park in 1886.

Military administration continued for thirty years, and soldiers enforced the rules and regulations, sometimes with zeal. They removed squatters, captured lawbreakers, hunted down poachers, burned illegal dwellings, and confiscated guns and traps. During this period roads, trails, and hotels were either built or improved. For want of a policy on national parks, however, hotels were located much too close to features the park was supposed to preserve. Park personnel also took from within the park the trees and rock they needed for construction purposes. Such acts seem primitive in light of present-day practice, but through such trial and error the Army sustained and carried forth the national park idea.

Nevertheless, there were some near disasters. Aubrey Haines, the distinguished park historian, feels that the only thing that saved Yellowstone from having a railroad built directly into the geyser basins was a financial panic that set back rail progress nationally for at least six years. By that time enough support had been gained for the national park idea to defeat the railroads, but only after a battle. A member of Congress summed up the matter in 1890: "I am opposed to granting any railway the right-of-way through the park because the first would only force the precedent for many which would follow."

One thing that helped, and has always helped, was the interest of influential people. The glowing reports of editors and authors, for example, nurtured a sense of national pride; the press exerted enormous force simply by informing the public of what was happening. Among the early authors who visited Yellowstone were Rudyard Kipling, Owen Wister, and Emerson Hough, and the first President to visit the park, Chester A. Arthur, came in 1883. James Garfield visited the park before becoming President. In 1903 Theodore Roosevelt spent two weeks in the park, accompanied by the famous naturalist John

Above: *Wading in pool at Great Fountain Geyser, 1908.* Left: *Tourists posing, 1922.* Below: *The debris removed from Morning Glory Pool in 1950 included over $90 in coins, 100 handkerchiefs, many towels, and various articles of clothing.*

Above: *The National Park Service attempted for many years to place wild animals on public exhibit. Rangers kept bison in a corral as a "show herd."* Right: *Garbage fed to bears at prearranged times lured many tourists, as in this 1936 view.* Far right: *Bear-feeding platform at Old Faithful, 1929. Public revulsion later led to elimination of such practices.*

Burroughs. "I cannot too often repeat," said Roosevelt, "that the essential feature in the present management of the Yellowstone Park . . . is its essential democracy . . . the preservation of the scenery, of the forests, of the wilderness life and the wilderness game for the people as a whole instead of leaving the enjoyment thereof to be confined to the very rich who can control private reserves." (In succeeding years, three other Presidents—Warren G. Harding, Calvin Coolidge, and Franklin D. Roosevelt—visited the park during their terms of office.)

Developing the Wilderness

The turn of the century was a very confusing time for the national park idea. Man simply had not adopted the philosophy of leaving things in their natural condition. In his anthropocentric view, the principal way to "correct" the inequities of nature was to divide wildlife into good animals or bad, and then get rid of the bad.

As so often happens, however, the lead in conservation progress came not from public officials but from private citizens, the majority of whom knew what they wanted Yellowstone not to be. They wanted it not to be a hunter's paradise, and eventually they became so indignant, especially at headhunters' taking bison heads to sell as trophies, that Congress finally passed a bill that did what the Yellowstone Act had failed to do. It clarified authority, jurisdiction, and penalties involving offenses committed within the park, and provided for the

assignment of a United States commissioner to handle court cases.

This gave strength to the law, but men had a great deal yet to learn about how to manage a national park. Some early park administrators, civilian as well as army, seldom remembered the mandate to keep Yellowstone's resources "in their natural condition." Or else they followed the principle of naturalness only within the limited framework of their knowledge. There are two glaring examples of how they ignored the principle: hotels and wildlife.

A congressional report in 1886 had urged that Yellowstone be spared the "vandalism of improvement" and went on to say of the park that "its great and only charms are in the display of wonderful forces of nature, the ever-varying beauty of the rugged landscape, and the sublimity of the scenery. Art can not embellish them." This was largely ignored. One of man's early acts was to construct a massive hotel 220 yards from the park's most famous thermal feature, Old Faithful Geyser. Not only was the design grandiose and pompous, as though the building were supposed to compete with the geyser for attention, but the 500 tons of stone required to build an eighty-five-foot-high fireplace in it came from within the park. Nowadays, hotels need not be built in national parks because rapid and comfortable transportation permits a visitor to enter and leave in a single day and thus spend the night outside the park. But in the early days it was a jolting, dusty ride by stagecoach or horseback even to get near the park, and then a perilous climb to the high plateaus to see the major features. Thus justified, hotels were built very near, if not nearly on top of, prominent features: the Lake Hotel 100 yards from the shore of Yellowstone Lake, and concessionary facilities within a few steps of the rim of the Grand Canyon of the Yellowstone River.

As for wildlife, some of the animals of Yellowstone suffered severe cruelties at the hands of men in the early days. Grizzly bear cubs were chained to posts at the hotels. Elk were kept in captivity in what were

Top: *Yellowstone was regarded by some early visitors as a paradise for unlimited hunting and fishing.* Bottom: *Elk hunting, circa 1897.*

nothing more than tourist zoos, where they had to endure extreme filth and eat slop and swill. Bears, being more omnivorous, fed in garbage cans and dumps and became indolent; in their enthusiasm for more of man's foods, they invaded campgrounds and hotels. From these places they had to be removed by one means or another.

Tons of fish were taken annually from Yellowstone Lake to serve the tourists. Some fishermen took out a hundred or so fish at a time, simply so they could be photographed with the catch. The Army itself was responsible for stocking streams with exotic rainbow, brown, brook, and lake trout and encouraging angling as a tourist attraction, often with adverse effects upon native trout. Perch and bass were introduced, but without success. Fishery stations were established at several points in the park, including the edge of Yellowstone Lake.

It is nothing less than a miracle that more fish did not accidentally enter the lake, multiply, and modify the original populations of native cutthroat trout. As it was, Atlantic salmon and rainbow trout were actually introduced into the lake. Fortunately, they failed to establish permanent populations. Over the years, however, several species of nonnative forage fish have accidentally been introduced into the lake, probably by bait fishermen, and they remain as a disrupting influence on the natural aquatic ecosystem.

Far from keeping Yellowstone's natural wonders "in their natural condition," some of the early administrators tried in various ways to "improve" the original character of the park. They felt, for example, that parts or all of the major wildlife herds should be fenced in, because otherwise they might die out. To make the park more interesting, the introduction of wild animals from other lands was proposed, and four chamois destined for Yellowstone actually got as far as Washington, D.C., before the project was cancelled.

Wildlife Management Begins

Despite mistakes and oversights, a great concept had begun to emerge. To the eternal credit of Yellow-

stone, it was here that the first attempts at wildlife management on any federal land took place. An air of urgency attended these efforts, mainly because of bison. Yellowstone had the last wild herd in the country; most mountain bison elsewhere had been slaughtered decades before. Even the bison living in the park when it was established were nearly eliminated by poachers, and some authorities became convinced that the animal's fate was sealed.

Top: *Pronghorn trapping operations in 1951 were intended to reduce the size of the herd.* Bottom: *Bison feeding operations in the Lamar Valley, 1933.*

This fear led to a crash program that was intended to restore the numbers of bison—but, alas, the result was that a different subspecies was introduced. These interbred with the native mountain species to produce a hybrid population. Moreover, herds were subjected to intense domestication, which included herding, haying, fencing, castration of calves, planting of crops, and digging of irrigation canals, as though the park were intended to be a kind of ranch. As a matter of fact, a "Buffalo Ranch" was established in the Lamar River Valley in 1907 and hay-feeding activities continued there for forty-five years.

In their concern to sustain existing population levels of certain animal species, early park officials decided to limit the capture of bison, deer, and elk by predators. A campaign to reduce or exterminate these predators was heartily approved by neighboring ranchers, who had been accusing park authorities of "running a coyote factory." So the Army began eliminating "bad" animals, with the help of packs of hounds. One by one the predators were reduced.

By 1906 mountain lions were almost gone, despite advice from President Theodore Roosevelt, who was well ahead of much contemporary biological thinking, in a letter to the park superintendent:

> *Dear General Young:*
>
> *I do not think any more cougars (mountain lions) should be killed in the park. Game is abundant. We want to profit by what has happened in the English preserves, where it proved to be bad for the grouse itself to kill off all the peregrine falcons and all the other birds of prey. It may be advisable, in case the ranks of the deer and antelope right around the Springs should be too heavily killed out, to kill some of the cougars there, but in the rest of the park I certainly would not kill any of them. On the contrary, they ought to be let alone.*

This stopped the slaughter, but only temporarily. The campaign resumed not long afterward and dozens of mountain lions were shot. Annual reports of park superintendents show that in two decades more than 111 lions and 50 wolves were destroyed. To make matters worse, official coyote poisoning began in 1895, and not even the establishment of the National Park Service in 1916 could quickly halt such long-established programs. Today we look with horror upon such proceedings, as often happens with the advantage of hindsight. But it must be remembered that the pioneer wildlife managers of those days were following the best available recommendations of science. The soldiers and rangers were rugged men who by and large conducted themselves superbly and at times even risked their lives to see that the park was protected and its wildlife undisturbed—a situation that prevails today. We have no reason to doubt that their procedures, however ill advised, were well intentioned. Indeed, we can only be grateful that their overall efforts helped bring ultimate success.

The National Park Service

While all this was going on, the national park idea began to gain support, and Congress, following the Yellowstone model, authorized the establishment of other national parks: Yosemite and Sequoia in California, Mount Rainier in Washington, Crater Lake in Oregon, Wind Cave in South Dakota, Mesa Verde and Rocky Mountain in Colorado, Platt in Oklahoma, and Glacier in Montana. The problem was that federal administration of this growing system was rather haphazard; therefore, in 1916 Congress established the National Park Service, a new federal bureau in the Department of the Interior, to bring the parks onto a firmer management basis.

The mission of this new organization, as stated in the act, was simple but contradictory:

> *The service thus established shall promote and regulate the use of the . . . national parks, monuments, and reservations . . . by such means and measures as conform to the fundamental purpose of the said parks . . . which purpose is to conserve the scenery and the natural and historic objects and the wild life therein and to provide for the*

enjoyment of the same in such manner and by such means as will leave them unimpaired for the enjoyment of future generations.

This sentence expressed perhaps the most important concept up to that time in the history of national park management. It spelled out a little more clearly what an earlier Congress meant when it directed Yellowstone's resources to be kept in their natural condition. Furthermore, the administration, protection, and promotion of other national parks were thereafter subjected directly to the provisions of this Act. The mandate to conserve became, above everything else, the mission of the National Park Service.

Yet in misguided efforts to save the bison and other ungulates, more than 134 wolves were shot in Yellowstone National Park in the first ten years after the National Park Service was established. After that there were only sporadic sightings of wolves, and some people felt that the animal had become extinct in the park.

No bird suffered more persecution in Yellowstone than the pelican. Its natural predilection for fish seemed to interfere with man's desire to enjoy superlative fishing in Yellowstone Lake, so when trout populations declined the pelican was blamed, although, ironically, man himself had collected and removed more than 200 million trout eggs from the lake. Between 1901 and 1953 a trout hatchery that was for a time the world's largest operated on the shore of Yellowstone Lake. Fish traps were placed on spawning streams that entered the lake, and eggs were collected and taken to the hatchery. The purpose of this extensive operation was to plant cutthroat trout in barren waters throughout the Rocky Mountains.

The extent of biological knowledge at the time was exceedingly limited, and the National Park Service was advised on the best authority to undertake control of the pelicans. The easiest and most effective way to reduce these birds was to land on the Molly Islands, in Yellowstone Lake, where they bred most abundantly, and remove their eggs. Between 1924 and 1932 hundreds of eggs were removed, and scores of young pelicans were killed. This activity soon came under attack by conservation societies, who published reports accusing the National Park Service of wrongdoing. Growing public pressure plus the mounting of scientific evidence as to the value of the bird to the ecosystem eventually led to the halting of pelican control in 1932.

The Tourist Flood

Meanwhile, travelers flocked to the region. Many rode the Northern Pacific Railway to its terminus outside the northern boundary and swarmed into the park by horse and buggy, stagecoach, wagon, bicycle, and, ultimately, automobile. To most of them the national park idea was still a hazy experiment. They knew that the Yellowstone country was protected in some way, and most of them behaved respectably when they wandered among its delicate thermal features and fragile forests.

The provision of public services for these visitors took different forms, chiefly overnight accommodations and public tours. Occasionally a hotel or transportation employee looked upon a particular visitor as an irritant and sometimes gave him cavalier treatment. The tourist was also subject to the peril of stagecoach wrecks and to price-gouging.

But the visitor was also to be served, and guides and rangers have always zealously tried to help visitors understand and appreciate the park. In the early years, however, there was a feeling that educational activities would keep people away. For that reason, stories told by pioneer drivers and guides left much to be desired—except in the realm of fantasy, for Yellowstone offered a wealth of opportunities to stretch the truth to the limit. For example, one story told by guides in the thermal basins was that the birds drank so much hot water they laid hard-boiled eggs.

This was often great fun, but visitors came to prefer the educational approach. After all, Yellowstone was an extraordinary assemblage of scientific phenomena. Recognizing the potential, the National Park Service soon organized a corps of well-trained, uniformed naturalists to interpret the language of the scientist into terms most people could understand. These "interpreters," whose work got its initial impetus in the early 1920's, gave lectures, took the public on guided tours, conducted evening programs, built museum exhibits, and produced pamphlets. Personable men and women in uniform added immense enjoyment and satisfaction to the visitor's stay and gave him a new appreciation of the park's features. Very often the summer "interpreters" were selected from highly competent teachers and professors in high schools or colleges, and it is not too much to say that they played an important role not only in imparting information but in building a national conscience of conservation.

Other attempts to provide public services were less enduring. Feeding garbage to bears became a major public attraction during the Army's administration of Yellowstone National Park. Later these "feeding shows" were supervised by the National Park Service. Garbage was placed on platforms, the bears came running, and people took pictures to their heart's content; or visitors went to garbage dumps to see the grizzlies rummage amid debris and eat their fill—devouring glass and cans in the process. Repugnance to this practice finally grew so strong that it was discontinued in 1941, but it had been carried on for twenty-two years.

As Yellowstone became more famous, the flood of tourists swelled. By 1900 the annual number of visitors reached nearly 9,000. After World War II it began a sharp rise, finally reaching and passing 2 million visitors a year in 1965. The impact of so many people became tremendous, especially since nearly 90 per cent of them arrived in June, July, and August. Today an average of 30,000 to 40,000 visitors are inside the national park each day during the summer, and the annual total is well above 2 million.

The Battle Over Elk

Another problem with which men dealt, almost in panic, was the fluctuating population of elk. Fearing that other Yellowstone ungulates would go the way of the bison toward a seeming extinction, the Army instituted feeding programs just before the turn of the century. People who saw some of the animals frozen and obliterated by prolonged cold and heavy winter snows, a process that had been going on for millenniums, felt compelled to "correct" the situation. Private citizens also became involved, for with reports of starving elk came calls from nearby cities to start a feeding program. People angrily asked why the Department of the Interior "allowed animals to die of starvation and not do all within their power to relieve this suffering." Pursuing such compassions, private citizens exerted extraordinary pressures on park staffs and state game management authorities.

There was little question that man had disrupted the elk's accustomed relation to its habitat. It was apparent that great numbers of livestock outside the park were removing some of the grass on which elk normally fed in winter. Human dwellings had proliferated so much that elk could no longer migrate into the lower reaches of the Yellowstone River without the risk of getting shot. Men reduced the predators that had normally cropped their share of elk each year. They also removed the Indians, halted hunting, and suppressed forest fires.

In misguided pity for wildlife, most people did not yet understand that the best way to maintain ungulates in a natural, healthy condition is to leave them alone and sustain the environmental conditions that originally produced them. It was difficult to keep in mind that all life is temporary, and that death by freezing, predation, and starvation, however "cruel," was normal and essential to the health of ungulates as a whole.

The feeding program initiated by the Army lasted for decades, and it was commonplace to see haystacks and fields of alfalfa in Yellowstone National Park. Later, at the height of the program, park

Top: Tourist group at Liberty Cap, 1888. Cottage and Mammoth Hotels in background. Bottom: President Chester A. Arthur and party in Yellowstone National Park, August, 1883. "Nothing I have ever read," said the President, "nothing I have ever heard, equals what I have seen."

Left: *Traveling through Yellowstone National Park was not always easy. This is the route between Norris and Madison Junction in 1917.* Below: *First automobiles to enter Yellowstone National Park over Sylvan Pass, July 4, 1915.* Right: *The transition in transportation is marked by this 1922 view of wagons and automobiles on the road near Madison Junction.* Far right: *Until park roads were improved, travelers had considerable trouble in rainy weather.*

rangers fed up to 900 tons of hay each year to the park's bison and other wildlife. Predator reduction continued with the poisoning of ungulate carcasses to get rid of more wolves and coyotes.

By the mid 1930's, however, biologists felt that the elk had multiplied out of all proportion to the range that was supposed to feed them, and the Lamar River Valley and much of the Yellowstone drainage, in their view, began to look like a field of battle across which wars had raged. They saw animals peeling bark and leaves off aspen trees and decried the loss of whole groves, which were turned into little more than barren poles and sticks. They reported pines and Douglas firs chewed off to the maximum height the animals could reach, rabbit-brush nibbled almost to the ground, sagebrush devoured excessively, and every available form of browse reduced below what they considered to be its normal productive capacity. All this, plus the grass being decimated, stones bared, and soil opened up to erosion, convinced wildlife managers that the Yellowstone flora was deteriorating because of too many ungulates. Quite probably, though they had no way of knowing it, this sort of thing had occurred naturally before man came. Nevertheless, they became convinced that the impact on the winter range had to be reduced.

In time an increasing segment of the public came to agree that perhaps there were too many elk on the range and that the overpopulation should be reduced. A vocal minority demanded that the park be opened to public hunting, something never envisioned in the national park idea. Attempts were made to trap the elk and take them away, but this could not be accomplished rapidly enough or on a large enough scale to be of much help. The reduction was finally carried out by rangers during the 1950's and early 1960's. Through the process of trapping, removing, and shooting, the northern herd was reduced to about 4,000 individuals by 1967.

In the end, men came to appreciate much better the delicate relationship between wild animals and their environment; they gained a more thorough understanding of the concepts of ecology, and began to review the policies of the past. Elk mortality, especially during severe winters, was accepted as a natural process. Shooting and poisoning of the "bad" animals were halted, and the surviving predators were assiduously guarded. Today park biologists administer a program designed to encourage the natural regulation of elk within the park and the re-establishment of historical winter migrations to lands outside Yellowstone. The National Park Service also refined and improved its statement of the primary purpose of Yellowstone National Park: to preserve natural ecosystems and provide opportunities for visitors to see and appreciate the natural scenery and native plant and animal life as it occurred in pristine America.

This was no more or less than what the Yellowstone Act in 1872, and the National Park Service Act of 1916, required. Preserving the natural ecosystem was still easier to say than to do, but at long last the decision was made to allow natural controls to operate as freely as possible, thereby permitting predators, scavengers, disease, and weather to take their normal toll.

Civilization Comes to Yellowstone

While these events were taking place, other parts of the Yellowstone ecosystem came to know the hand of man. Telephone lines crisscrossed the park. Construction materials for roads were dug from some fifty gravel pits. Airplanes flew over the park with minimum restrictions, frightening wildlife. Rangers captured animals for shipment to zoos. Scientists conducting research affixed plasticized nylon tags in combinations of red, orange, blue, green, or white to the ears of wild animals, and even attached radio transmitters to grizzly bears.

During the 1930's a heavy loss of whitebark pine to mountain pine beetles caused such a panic that 4,000 trees were cut on Mount Washburn. In 1957 airplanes sprayed DDT over the Yellowstone River drainage in an attempt to control spruce budworm. The result was a die-off and subsequent alteration of invertebrate populations in the Yellowstone; DDT was found in trout eighty-five miles below the spray area, and fish taken more than two years after spraying were found to contain DDT.

Nonnative grass was planted to "green up" embankments of roads within the park, and periodically from high levels of administration came suggestions for fencing a few bears and bison so that visitors could see them more readily. A show corral on Antelope Creek, on the north slope of Mount Washburn, contained bison from the mid-1930's until after World War II, when the fence was removed. Men constructed in the Park, among other things, 750 miles of roads, 1,159 miles of trails, 2,100 buildings, 7 amphitheaters, 24 water systems, 30 sewer systems, 10 electric systems with 93 miles of transmission lines, 13 dumps, 54 picnic areas, 3,143 campsites, 47 outdoor interpretive devices, and 17,000 signs.

Thus, in Yellowstone's first century, countless attempts were made to try out the national park idea and see if nature could be improved upon. But the principal victims of such "improvement" were the plants, the animals, and the wilderness environment. From the hands of poachers, tourists, soldiers, scientists, and rangers the animals suffered hardships and change, and not until recently did the realization come to the National Park Service that the best kind of management—if it were possible after all the changes—was no management at all. Burgeoning conservation organizations had called for such action —or perhaps it would be better to say inaction—all along and even threatened to go to court over what they considered malpractices.

A governmental entity is apt to be both product and victim of the political system that nurtures it, for the funds that give it life are authorized and appropriated by political bodies. According to the accustomed rhetoric, the more constituents that can be served by an appropriation, the better. This principle once led to the maxim that "parks are for people," a phrase interpreted by some people to be another threat to the national park idea. "What it means," one eminent conservationist told us, "is that parks are for motors, with people on them."

The idea of parks being primarily for people quickly came under fire, partly because millions of people were already swarming into and overcrowding the nation's scenic treasures, and partly because a great many citizens themselves felt that national parks should be for animals of all kinds, man included. In fact, the feeling has grown rather strong that if there must be an ultimate choice, the rights of animals in the parks transcend those of man. In the words of Dr. Raymond Dasmann, a conservationist of world renown, "National parks were set aside to preserve unique and irreplaceable natural environments. . . . Where people conflict with the goal of preservation of these unique natural environments people must be excluded."

This seems to be the direction in which world opinion is moving, too. A catalogue of errors committed in Yellowstone is useful, but of greater importance is the manner in which the United States has corrected those errors and made sure that they will not be repeated or compounded. Longer than any other national park, Yellowstone has been a testing ground for the national park idea. The fact that this park has largely remained in a natural condition after all the trial and error, the depredations, and "vandalism of improvement" is a tribute to the viability of the park and its wild creatures. It is also a tribute to those rangers and naturalists in the past who counseled great care in the management of wildlife, who insisted on keeping the wildness free of intruding facilities, and whose views were not always heeded.

Back to Nature

Even with budgets that frequently proved inadequate, park officials set up a protection that has evolved, if painfully, into what seems at last a sound amalgam of conservation management and public use. Structures are now being torn down, dumps and gravel pits abandoned, former roads obliterated, human uses that compete with nature transferred outside the park, pollution reduced, and original wild conditions restored as much as possible.

No longer are fragments of geyser cones permitted to be taken out of the park. The bathhouses of old have long since been torn down and the waters restored to their natural channels and left to flow freely. No person is allowed to swim in a thermal spring or cast any object whatever—including soap—into it. The railroad companies that once threatened to invade the park abandoned the idea years ago. Construction of hotels and other urban features has been reduced to a minimum or curtailed entirely.

Grizzly bear cubs are no longer chained to posts. Any harassment of animals is strictly forbidden. Spraying pesticides has been discontinued. Limits have been set on how many fish may be taken from the water and kept. Fish from the park are not utilized for hotel dinner tables in the park or anywhere else. No new exotic fish are permitted in park waters, and the streams and lakes are being restored wherever possible to conditions resembling those that prevailed before the park was established.

In short, artificiality is being removed. The park education program has expanded and been refined. The National Park Service believes that its goal in Yellowstone, in ecological terms, is to preserve the natural relationships between an interacting biota (flora and fauna) and its environment. If human influences become detrimental to the environment, the activities of human visitors, rather than those of native wildlife, will have to change.

So advanced does this concept appear to be that the national park idea may well be on the verge of coming of age. The belief now is that ungulate populations in the northern Rocky Mountain region historically have been regulated by a combination of natural factors, including severe winter weather, temporary deficiencies in the quality or quantity of food, predation, scavenging, parasites, and disease.

*Public services began early.
Right: In this 1903 view,
a soldier conducts park visitors in the geyser basins.
Left: Patrol by horseback,
1903. Below left: Park
ranger on motorcycle, 1923.
Below: Group of drivers and
coaches.*

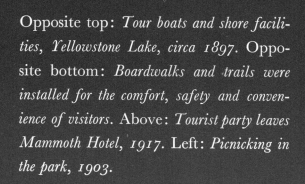

Opposite top: *Tour boats and shore facilities, Yellowstone Lake, circa 1897.* Opposite bottom: *Boardwalks and trails were installed for the comfort, safety and convenience of visitors.* Above: *Tourist party leaves Mammoth Hotel, 1917.* Left: *Picnicking in the park, 1903.*

Outside interference or intensive artificial management programs can disrupt the normal functioning of the ecosystem, and cause the animals to shy away from human beings, a process known as conditioned avoidance. On the other hand, the Madison elk herd has demonstrated that animals are relatively unaffected by large numbers of visitors viewing or photographing them.

Biologists are also convinced that affording visitors opportunities to see wild grizzly bears in natural surroundings is a responsibility that can be carried out with reasonable safety to man and bear. They foresee daily monitoring of grizzly activities so that preventive management can be undertaken if trouble approaches. Human uses of the park, they think, can be adapted to the needs of the grizzly rather than the other way around.

Perhaps the greatest testimonial to positive human efforts is the fact that not a single species of plant or animal originally found by man in the Yellowstone has been exterminated. Though the relative abundance of certain species may have shifted, everything is still there. Partly this is because life itself is tenacious. Yet man has recognized that ecosystems are fragile, and Yellowstone National Park represents a turning point where man's resolve to conserve has taken precedence over his ability to destroy.

This is a landmark of the first magnitude. Few animals other than man consciously protect or rescue their own kind, as the walrus does. Fewer yet protect other kinds. None saves whole ecosystems; that is a distinctly human trait. During much of the history of man as a species, preservation has been submerged among his instincts for hunting. The protection principle emerged occasionally, as in the writings of such persons as Cicero, but not until the Yellowstone experience did men ever undertake to conserve so large a piece of nature. Not until Yellowstone did

men attempt to protect all parts of an immense series of ecosystems. Even now it is a little difficult to grasp how the early explorers, the Army, the park men, and the public embraced the national park idea so fully and worked at it with such diligence and dedication that the parks were ultimately threatened by too large a number of visitors.

The present popularity of national parks suggests that they have become more than refuges for men to retreat to from a society that moves too fast or from environments that are no longer clean. The national park idea may have helped to open an era in which man will develop a thorough environmental awareness and in which he will check his technological prowess and impose limits upon himself. It has already been suggested that economic development be slowed or halted in certain fields and that population controls be instituted among human beings. If nothing else, the national parks are glimpses of what the pristine environment was and could be again. Yellowstone has survived man's attempts to regulate it and therein lies a hope that Thomas Edison was right when he said that what man's mind can create, man's character can control.

So far, the national park idea has undergone a gestation period, a birth in 1872, and a hundred-year history of youth. Now it is maturing. Men still experiment with it. Another century, we may hope, will see improvements so profound as to make the centennial of 1972 seem only a step on the road to a more sensitive, comprehensive human enjoyment and understanding of the natural world.

In the meantime, the national park idea has become universally popular and spread far beyond the borders of the United States. It has, in fact, caught on so thoroughly that national parks have multiplied beyond any dream of the men who fought to establish Yellowstone.

Top: *Recreational vehicle, 1924 style.* Bottom: *Public campground at Mammoth, 1922.*

10

The Idea Spreads

Here the world is still young and fragile, held in trust for your sons and ours.

Sign at the entrance to
Serengeti National Park, Tanzania, Africa

With all the challenges Yellowstone faced, it is little wonder that the national park idea spread slowly. Indeed, attempts to repeal the Yellowstone Act might have succeeded if the sentiment for conservation had been a little less strong. A park on Mackinac Island, Michigan, was authorized by Congress in 1875 but it is no longer a national park. In fact, the next national park in the United States was not set aside for sixteen years.

Several other countries picked up the idea, however, soon after word of the Yellowstone experiment spread, and modified the process of park establishment in interesting ways. Whereas nearly all of Yellowstone's original Indian inhabitants were driven out by the newcomers, the opposite of this occurred in New Zealand. An association of Maori chiefs headed by Te Heuheu Tukino presented to the government in 1887 a nucleus of land that was the first private donation in history specifically for national park purposes. Seven years later it was made into Tongariro National Park. Perito Moreno, an Argentine scientist-explorer, made a similar donation in 1903 when he turned over a grant of land in the heart of the Andes for the purpose of establishing Nahuel Huapí National Park, now the largest and most popular in Argentina.

In 1875, the United States Congress, in its authorization of Mackinac Island, adopted the term "national public park, or grounds," but the first time the words "national park" were used in the body of a public act was in the establishment of Royal National Park, near Sydney, Australia, in 1879. It was then called simply "the National Park." (The first legislative reference to Yellowstone as a national park occurred in 1883 in a bill relating to appropriations.) Canada established its first, Banff National Park, in the province of Alberta in 1887.

Despite these developments, the movement gained little momentum. Much of the world's population lived outdoors anyway and it was hard for such people to see the point in "locking up" natural resources from which they had to make a living or

Ecuador: Galápagos National Park, South Plaza Island.

against which they sometimes fought for survival. Alligators and crocodiles were a menace to man, so the thinking went, and of course had very useful hides, so the reptiles were extensively utilized—and nearly exterminated from certain major rivers. Anyone who wanted to protect jaguars must have seemed mad to the primitive mind; the numbers of jaguars and jungle parrots seemed inexhaustible to early people. And such must have seemed the status of wildebeests, vicuñas, koalas, rhinos, passenger pigeons. . . .

The usual commercial opponents of wild land conservation—the petroleum interests, agriculture, heavy industry—succeeded in delaying as many park proposals as possible so that the resources could be exploited, and where they failed to delay the forces of conservation they made those forces seem to be opposed to colonists, the poor, and "progress." These arguments had a grave effect. In Africa the national parks established by colonial administrations were viewed in certain quarters as private preserves for rich white men. Almost universally, high government officials insisted that national parks produce prompt economic returns or be put to "more productive" uses. This policy placed pressure on the national parks, as it had in Yellowstone, because approach roads and facilities had to be built and public services offered before much profit could be obtained from tourism.

No country had a plan for establishing an orderly system of reserves that would include all the most important ecosystems. None even had an inventory of natural resources. In the United States the parks grew helter-skelter, dependent partly on which member of Congress worked the hardest or had the greatest influence. Yosemite National Park was authorized in 1890, but only as an unmanaged, doughnut-shaped reserve surrounding the original federal grant to the state; the park as we know it today was established much later, when California ceded its grant back to the federal government. Twelve more years went by with only Mount Rainier established as a

national park, and in that case, too, there was a lack of firm and immediate management. By the turn of the century the only other countries that had established park systems were Australia, New Zealand, Canada, and Mexico.

Not until transportation had improved and automobiles had been widely accepted did the movement gain strength. The automobile helped "democratize" the parks; it made them available to all people rather than only to the carriage trade—persons able to afford the long, expensive travels previously required to reach such parks as Yellowstone. A local promotional scheme called the "park-to-park highway" was organized to encourage travel. It remained clear, however, that national parks were not set aside primarily for tourism but rather to preserve the outstanding natural heritage of the country. One eminent proponent of this philosophy was John Muir, whose writings were becoming increasingly popular; he counseled appreciation of the land for its own sake rather than for commercial profit.

Sweden established a group of parks in 1909, but by and large the priceless natural treasures of the world were placed under protection one at a time: Iguazú Falls in Argentina, a portion of the Swiss Alps, the gorilla country of the African Congo, the Cambodian ruins of Angkor Wat, the deserts of southern Africa. Many, if not most, of these began as Yellowstone did—remote, seldom visited, endangered. Iguazú Falls, in the subtropical forest near where Argentina, Brazil, and Paraguay meet, is hard to reach even today. But it was early recognized as one of the natural wonders of Latin America, and perhaps the most magnificent waterfall in the Western Hemisphere. The flow of its 278 thundering cataracts is less than that of Niagara Falls, but its surroundings are still in a fairly wild state. It conforms to the national park idea because it is not composed of falls alone, just as Yellowstone is not composed of geysers alone; it is an ecosystem of many parts. Spray leaps high in the air above the Throat of the Devil, a seething, roaring cauldron of white foaming water at the base of a semicircular system of falls. Great flocks of wild green parrots circle overhead. Deep in the dense green forest chattering *boyeros*, a kind of blackbird, build their nests. Air plants gleam with an intense translucent red under the white-hot sun. In the woods one finds an old Guaraní woman and is reminded of some of the richest folklore and most interesting love songs in the world.

Iguazú is as unique as Yellowstone. And it has problems as drastic as those at Old Faithful or Yellowstone Lake, for on the Brazilian side a huge purple hotel has been constructed on the brink of the Iguazú River Gorge. This edifice has stimulated pressure on Argentine authorities to build the same kind of facilities on their side. They have splendid accommodations, ten miles away in the subtropical forest, but planners in the tourist industry prefer a hotel right on the brink of the natural feature the park was meant to conserve.

As plainly idealistic and altruistic as the national park idea is, it has been fought by private-interest groups in almost every country. Urban, agricultural, and power development schemes have encroached on prime national heritage lands, and commercial over-exploitation has threatened wild animal life. The notion of national parks has been disturbing to animal exporters in the Amazon, for example, and to poachers in Africa, who believe that the animals are there for everyone to hunt and take. But governments have slowly begun to realize that if an adequate number of sanctuaries are not provided, important animal species will disappear.

Thus Albert National Park was established in the Congo to protect the forest home of the mountain gorilla. Some parks were named after the primary species of plants or animals they were designed to protect: Wood Buffalo in Canada; Addo Elephant, Bontebok, and Mountain Zebra in South Africa; Los Alerces and El Palmar in Argentina.

More common, of course, has been the practice of naming national parks for their central scenic feature, such as Mayon Volcano in the Philippines, one of the most symmetric and beautiful mountains in the world. The highest peaks on each continent have not always been included. Mount Everest (Asia) and Mount Aconcagua (South America) are so inaccessible that they could scarcely qualify under the principle that national parks are for the benefit and enjoyment of all the people, although they otherwise merit consideration. Mount McKinley (North America), Kilimanjaro (Africa), and Mount Kosciusko (Australia) did qualify, for enough surrounding terrain could be incorporated to provide a treasure of enduring experiences for human visitors. One sight of a flock of crimson rosellas flying over a snowfield in Kosciusko National Park makes the true Australia come alive, makes "national park" mean something special again.

The Golden Ages

Hundreds of the outstanding natural features of the world are now protected to varying degrees through designation as national parks, including Mount Fujiyama in Japan, the volcanoes of Iztaccihuatl and Popocatepetl in Mexico, the "sugarloaf" domes and peaks around Rio de Janeiro in Brazil, Tierra del Fuego in Argentina, and the Serengeti Plains of Africa. The world's highest waterfall, Angel Falls, is in Canaima National Park, Venezuela.

Numerous sites received protection during the first great golden age of national parks in the 1930's. By then the fame of Yellowstone had spread, and the pace of the park movement had quickened. The Grand Canyon and Carlsbad Caverns, both internationally famous, had become national parks and the refinement of the United States system led other nations to adopt similar criteria for selecting and managing parks. Among these criteria were: a variety of outstanding landscapes in the national park system; each park of sufficient size to be easily manageable; adequate protection by rangers; good roads and trails; educational facilities; and accessibility to all citizens regardless of color, creed, or national origin.

Overleaf: Argentina: Iguazú National Park, Iguazú Falls.

The Japanese, particularly, paid a compliment to the American system by following its pattern. Other countries did likewise, though not so much duplicating the United States principle as adopting its best ideas and improving on them. Australia, Mexico, and the Philippines set up national parks during the 1930's, and even in the most remote areas of Africa the extraordinary wildlife resources began to receive protection. Europe seemed unlikely to have any areas wild enough and large enough to set aside, but Ireland, Italy, Finland, and Rumania joined the movement.

World War II temporarily slowed this progress and threatened to engulf some parks or lead to the exploitation of their resources for military purposes. But most parks survived the war and suffered only from severe neglect. After that the torrent of tourists started again, accompanied by so rapid a rise in foreign and domestic travel that tourism became the world's primary item of trade—and potential danger to the parks.

Yugoslavia established several reserves in 1949. It also showed unusual foresight in land use by passing a national law restricting the number of goats to two per family. Africans moved rapidly in the 1950's, another golden decade for the park idea, by setting up Serengeti National Park, Tanzania; Kafue National Park, Zambia; Aberdare National Park, Kenya; three large parks in Uganda; and others. Indeed, in 1958 the largest park in the world was established: Etosha National Park in South-West Africa. Its 16 million acres, combined with a surrounding buffer zone, equals a total protected area of nearly 40 million acres. That is nineteen times the size of Yellowstone, larger than the entire national park system of the United States, and comparable in size to one half of the state of Montana or two thirds of the British Isles.

Yellowstone thus is no longer the largest national park; at this writing it ranks seventeenth in size, and there are several of greater size about to be established, especially in Australia and in the Congo

Republic. The United States possesses a system of some 300 national parks and similar reserves (wildlife refuges, wilderness areas), the largest number in the world, but it no longer boasts the highest percentage of land thus reserved. Botswana has set aside 17 per cent of its total land surface as national parks and equivalent reserves. New Zealand and Dahomey have similarly protected 8 per cent of their territory, and so on down the list to the United States, which ranks eighth with only 3 per cent. Yellowstone, however, will always remain the place where the national park idea was crystallized and embodied in formal legislation.

Getting Together

The national park idea did not, of course, advance in a vacuum; other conservation efforts helped to further it. International agreements on fur seals and migratory birds provided landmarks on the road to wildlife conservation. The Society for the Preservation of the Fauna of the Empire was established in London in 1903, the International Committee for Bird Protection in 1922. At a Conference on Protection of African Fauna and Flora in London in 1933, initial attempts were made to clarify the differences between national parks and other kinds of reserves. Conservation foundations were established in the United States, Belgium, Poland, Germany; conservation laws were enacted in Germany, Denmark, Finland, Italy, Norway, Spain, and so on.

Thus far, three organizations exceedingly effective in the preservation of national parks and wildlife have been the Food and Agricultural Organization of the United Nations; the International Union for the Conservation of Nature and Natural Resources, organized in 1948 under the aegis of the United Nations; and the World Wildlife Fund, which began in 1961 to launch world-wide appeals for funds to save endangered animal species as well as habitats.

All this gave new impetus to the drive to establish national parks, and with the rapid increase in world tourism, government leaders were more and more

Tanzania: Serengeti National Park, zebra and wildebeest
at a water hole.

attracted to the idea. They heeded reports of American economists who calculated that national parks contribute millions, perhaps even billions, of dollars a year to the sales of firms throughout the nation, and generate many millions of dollars in income through personal services. Long before such figures were obtained, however, national leaders had begun to discover that making parks of their land and wildlife treasures did not mean isolation or loss of revenue, as a few people complained; rather they preserved the nation's character and produced substantial income in a way that would not use up or destroy the resources.

Accordingly, the Yellowstone experience was repeated hundreds of times. Australia and Great Britain brought their lists of national parks and similar reserves to nearly seventy-five, Canada and the U.S.S.R. to fifty, Poland, Malagasy, and Bulgaria to thirty, and Japan to twenty-five. New Zealand made national parks of its famed Mount Cook, its fiord-fringed coasts, and its finest and deepest lakes. Guatemala set aside its lovely Lake Atitlán, which is ringed with volcanic peaks and populated with descendants of the Maya Indians. One of the last wild homes of the tiger became Kanha National Park in India. Turkey, Thailand, Finland, and the Philippines organized one park after another. The United States established tropical parks in the Virgin Islands and Hawaii, and protected the Florida Everglades, the last undisturbed subtropical wilderness in the country. It also conferred on two areas park status that was long overdue, the California redwoods and the North Cascades. Of course, not all of these areas are fully protected or adequately planned and managed, but in time they are likely to be.

By 1972 the number of national parks and similar reserves in the world had risen to well over 1,200 in more than 100 countries. If Cook and Folsom, Washburn, Hedges, Hayden, and their colleagues were alive they would no doubt be astonished at how far their idea had traveled. George Catlin many times over would have had his hopes fulfilled for a "nation's park." Thoreau would be pleased to see how international has become his notion that in wildness is the preservation of the world, and John Muir would not be surprised to see the men of so many nations doing what Yellowstone and other wild places had inspired him to do: climb the mountains and get their good tidings.

The Pulse of Life

There are extraordinary good tidings to be had in national parks around the world. The bell-like song of the oropendola bird interrupts the hush of the Amazon forest and echoes with notes that seem to have a celestial origin. Hearing this is an experience almost identical to that of hearing the call of the sandhill crane in woods and marshes of Yellowstone. No two forests could differ more, but the effect upon man is the same: surprise, a stunning appreciation of wild music, a revelation of immensity, the realization of man's place not as conqueror but as sharer of the universe.

On the Caribbean shore of Costa Rica we swam over rich coral reefs unmarred by man, and afterward, drying off, walked under the coconut palms and listened to three wild symphonies at once: the skittering, rustling, scurrying of light-footed orange crabs beneath the fallen leaves; shrieks of bright green parrots flying over; and waves of drumlike grunts emanating for miles along the forested shore as howler monkeys raised a wilderness chorus. All this is now part of the Costa Rican national park system.

We hiked along wilderness trails in Khao Yai National Park, deep in the interior of Thailand, watched flame-colored minivets flit out over the rippling streams, studied tiger tracks made only hours before, and watched the movements of hornbills as they flew from tree to tree at sunset, going to roost. Khao Yai has road signs Yellowstone could never have: Caution: Elephant Crossing and Caution: Cobra Crossing.

Turkey: Pamukkale National Park, oleanders blooming on hot springs deposits.

No two national parks are alike. We felt a familiar sense of silence and wonder when caoeing among waterlogged woods in Kuscenneti ("bird paradise") National Park in Turkey; pelicans nested in treetops and wild white spoonbills winged like speeding clouds through the deep blue sky or chattered in the trees. It was not unlike the night we drifted silently by canoe into the Caroni Swamp in Trinidad and listened to an almost deafening racket as scarlet ibises flew in to roost. No park is the same as another; yet there is a oneness in the universe that each displays and to which each is linked.

We remembered Yellowstone's superlative thermal features when we stood on the flank of Mount Tongariro in New Zealand. At that place the same feeling of one-world unity was inescapable; above us roared the vents of Ketetahi Hot Springs shooting clouds of steam high into the air, and just beyond—accentuating the immense energies within the earth—lay the smoking summit of Ngauruhoe Volcano.

The most memorable experience we have ever had with wildlife was in Galápagos National Park. These volcanic islands of Ecuador that so influenced Charles Darwin in his researches in 1835 and thereafter are still mostly undisturbed. As we climbed or slid over broken lava we were reminded of the lava plateaus of Yellowstone, but there was a tremendous difference. In the Galápagos we had to watch where we walked, lest we step on mockingbirds or albatrosses. Land iguanas waddled between our legs. Sea lion bulls charged if we approached their harems too closely. Blue-footed boobies perched within arm's reach, looking at us as we looked at them. We could almost have reached up and touched a Galápagos hawk, one of the rarest birds in the world. Finches sang in cactuses and palo santo trees, undisturbed by our being close enough to pick them up. Nowhere had we felt so overwhelmingly that all animals were equals and associates on this planet. As in Yellowstone, we had once more touched a strange, unfathomable pulse of life in the wilderness lands of the world.

Extending the Park Idea

Parallel with national park development has been the establishment of reserves to protect endangered or vanishing species. Peru, for example, took an extraordinary step in 1966 when it established the 17,000-acre Pampas Galeras National Vicuña Reserve in the Andes. Though the land was remote and at a high elevation, men still encroached on the delicate vicuña's fragile habitat, killed the animals, took their hides, and sold the valuable fur in commercial markets. Establishing the reserve was a vexing experience for the Peruvians, but they made the project work by assigning and equipping guards, building employee housing, and securing the cooperation of local villagers. The vicuñas increased, but so did well-financed poachers with high-powered rifles, and the crisis is by no means over.

Increasingly, such projects are the result of cooperative efforts. In this case the Peruvians received assistance from the United States Peace Corps and the Food and Agricultural Organization of the United Nations. But sometimes there is a danger that priceless areas will be looked upon as public domain, and a country's citizens may feel that their sovereignty is threatened by tourists who overrun their parks. Some people say that the Galápagos Islands belong to all mankind, a sort of *tierra de nadie*, or no man's land. Esthetically, this may seem as correct for the Galápagos as for Yellowstone, and as national parks they are available to all men. But it should not be forgotten that Galápagos National Park belongs to the Republic of Ecuador.

In an increasing number of cases, the national park idea has been enlarged to include outstanding historic and archaeological sites. Such historic American sites as Independence Hall, the Statue of Liberty, Gettysburg Battlefield, and Fort Laramie are administered by the National Park Service. Turkey protects in Ephesus National Park the ancient Roman capital and center of Christianity where the disciples John and Paul lived and where the final home of the Virgin Mary has been located. Turkey

Switzerland: Swiss National Park.

has an abundance of ancient treasures and has already planned a substantial number of them as national parks: the capital of the Hittite Empire, the caves of Christian monks at Göreme, and the "overlaid" cities of ancient Troy.

Jordan established a national park at Jericho, in the Holy Land, and at the Qumran caves where the Dead Sea Scrolls were found. In Ancient Olympia National Park, Greece commemorates the site of the first Olympic games. At Tikal National Park, Guatemala preserves the largest of the Maya ruins. And in parks that are primarily natural, historic sites are carefully preserved—as in the case of a soldier station at Yellowstone or an old grist mill in the Great Smoky Mountains of Tennessee.

Problems of National Parks

Despite all these apparent successes, there are still difficulties that sometimes seem insurmountable. In addition to problems similar to those faced at Yellowstone, many countries are being confronted with bizarre and disastrous dangers that Yellowstone never endured.

Once national parks are established, there are sure to be proposals to excise parts of them, just as the northern part of Yellowstone was sought as a place to build a railroad. A recent example is La Vanoise National Park, France's first, where a proposal was made to remove for winter sports purposes 6,000 acres from the heart of the park, one of the most beautiful sections of the Alps and the main refuge of the ibex.

Whereas battles against railroad intrusion in Yellowstone were successful, other parks were not so fortunate. Although it is now abandoned, a railroad was thrust into Grand Canyon National Park. In Canada, transcontinental rails pass through the heart of Banff and Jasper national parks.

The United States happily has no aerial tramways in its national parks, but this precedent has been broken in Canada, Venezuela, and Turkey. Travelers occasionally enjoy some thrilling views from such sky rides, but the damage is incalculable: destruction of forest, introduction of artificiality on the horizon, and most of all, disruption of the spell of naturalness. Modern paved roads are not much better, but at least they can be made to blend with the landscape.

As in nineteenth-century Yellowstone, plans for the establishment of a national park in a developing country of the twentieth century spurs a rush by homesteaders to stake out private property. These squatters take over intended parklands so as to receive a high compensation when forced to relinquish the land. And governments no longer feel they can summarily eject a family or bulldoze a human habitation—not even one that has been illegally constructed.

In Costa Rica, where voting is compulsory and the poor have considerable political influence, twenty-eight families of squatters in Santa Rosa National Park were relocated within six days during 1970. Park authorities, using jeeps, oxcarts, and horses, conveyed the squatters and their possessions to an agricultural colony where each received a house and seventy-five acres of land, and where part of their food was supplied for six months by an agency of the United Nations. All this required the collaboration of ten governmental agencies and a cost to the Costa Rican National Park Service of $16,000. But the process smoothed the way for the opening of the park to the public the following year.

All this is not to say that the poor are unwelcome visitors to national parks. Quite the contrary, it is a concern of park directors to make the wonders and refreshing experiences in national parks available to all, and special efforts are frequently made to bring to the parks persons who cannot afford to get there by themselves. This is done by schools, service clubs, international agencies, and similar organizations.

Quite often a national park is established, just as Yellowstone was, without provision for law enforcement personnel, so poaching is a problem. In some instances oil reserves have proved a threat. Colombia is fighting to save the Macarena Reserve, a tropical mountain region rich in wildlife, for a national park. But no fewer than five petroleum companies have planned the exploitation of this undisturbed massif not far from the capital city of Bogotá, and have already constructed roads and started to take out wood, furs, and fish, presumably to produce some profit until the oil starts flowing. Park officials are hard pressed to combat the arguments of petroleum engineers and of lawyers in public ministries who say: "This country is poor and its people are dying from hunger. The only solution is money—and the oil of the Macarena means money."

Such promoters forget that tourism is a non-consumptive industry; little if anything would have to be extracted from the Macarena to satisfy the needs of a properly regulated travel industry. Moreover, should other sources of energy be developed, the world's dependence on oil may decline. Yet there seems to be little sign of travel declining, especially at Yellowstone, which should be a lesson in itself.

Another problem men never had to overcome in Yellowstone was destruction caused by international war. No battle ever erupted in Yellowstone to match the one that devastated Garamba National Park in the Congo in 1963. The region had for years been isolated, and had suffered intensive poaching as well as inroads by merchants attempting illegally to obtain ivory and rhinoceros horn. The park was established to try to restore disastrously dwindling numbers of giraffes and white rhinos. A biological research station located there had been of tremendous help, and the park's rare animals were slowly making a comeback. Then came civil war, and Congolese rebels invaded from the Sudan, occupying the northeastern section of the Congo. They sacked the headquarters buildings, destroyed the research station, massacred all of its animals, and moved into the park in an orgy of killing and collecting, leaving untold numbers of carcasses to rot. By the time government forces reached the region and repelled the rebels, wildlife had been driven from at least three-quarters of the park. Congolese authorities are

now rebuilding the animal populations and have made much progress. A recent wildlife census in the park showed that there were 251 white rhinos, 589 giraffes, 150 lions, 129 roan antelopes, and thousands of elephants and buffalo. "I am optimistic," the director of parks told us. "The Congo has established four new national parks, two of which total twelve million acres. We are trying to keep this one of the most beautiful countries in the world." Unfortunately, raids across the border from the Sudan continue to pose a problem. Rangers have been shot and killed by poachers in Congo parks and in the parks of other countries as well. That is something Yellowstone has been spared.

Perhaps the most imperilled reserve in the world is Galápagos National Park, for it lacks a sufficient number of rangers to enforce the law. We anchored one day off Espumilla Beach and while going ashore in a launch saw a small boat some distance down the shore depart in haste. A few moments later, behind the mangrove-covered dunes, we found a lagoon torn up for its salt deposits, and garbage scattered along the shores. Usually a flock of twenty flamingos inhabited that lagoon; only four remained, and no one knew whether the others had been frightened away or killed.

Far more serious are the devastating activities of exotic animals introduced by man. On San Salvador (James) Island alone there are 1,000 burros, 3,000 pigs, and 25,000 goats. The pigs open up what was hitherto impenetrable forest, and then the goats enter; by the time they are done, the landscape resembles a barren desert. "In all my time here," the chief park ranger told us, "I have never observed any of our giant tortoises less than fifteen years old. The pigs feed on their eggs and on the little tortoises. Last year we found fifty nests destroyed by pigs."

And yet, as in Yellowstone, there are remarkable instances around the world where men are meeting the challenges and turning their parks into signal successes. One of the most difficult and costly steps is the restoration of natural conditions. This often requires the removal not only of settlers but of an immense clutter of houses and other marks of civilization. For example, at Isla de Salamanca National Park, on the Caribbean coast, Colombian authorities have removed 226 private dwellings as well as eighty miles of fencing.

Yet the costs and efforts of such actions are worthwhile. In East Africa, where tourist travel is based largely on national parks, the annual growth rate of tourism is 15 per cent. Establishment of national parks and similar reserves helps to arrest the decay and ruin of such historic places as ancient Olympia, where the first Olympic games were held. Many areas are credited with the saving of animals from what seemed certain extinction, as in the case of the square-lipped rhinoceros in the Umfolozi and Hluhluwe game reserves of South Africa. Finally, in addition to their economic, historic, and wildlife values, the parks have preserved scarce open spaces in crowded, industrial countries like Japan and the Netherlands.

New Parks in the Offing

Despite all the progress, there are still some glaring omissions from the world's systems of national parks. For example, far too little of the Amazon Basin is included in national parks. Many Australians believe that their entire Great Barrier Reef, 1,250 miles long—not just small portions of it as at present—should be a national park. Beautiful and fragile portions of the Caribbean, especially coral banks and white sand beaches, are inadequately preserved. The Pacific Islands have splendid natural areas so remote as almost to be forgotten, yet deserving of protection before irreparable harm occurs from unplanned tourism or overexploitation. North Africa could have immense national parks in its desert regions.

The pace of setting up national parks is almost frenetic in certain countries. Belatedly, in fact almost too late, some citizens and their governments have realized that their greatest attractions are not casinos or avenues of hotels or racetracks or spas, but the unique natural and historic places that their countries possess. Alas, some forests have already nearly perished, like the Cedars of Lebanon, a tiny remaining patch of which the Republic of Lebanon guards as though the wood were gold. Some animals have perished, too, like the California grizzly. But Yellowstone has set an example for the preservation of total ecosystems. National parks are not trees alone, or animals alone; they should sustain whole natural systems or complete historic ideas.

Thus it is that Yellowstone fostered a global network of national parks whose intrinsic value no man can measure. That such a seemingly simple idea could sweep so far and penetrate so deeply the consciousness of other cultures is due in no small measure to the sense of national pride it ignited and sustained in the hearts of men.

Japan: Fuji-Hakone-Izu National Park, Mount Fujiyama.

The Next Hundred Years

11

The supreme triumph of parks is humanity.

ENOS MILLS

The sun had burst over the edge of the jagged peaks by the time we arrived at the mouth of the Val Trupchun. Light flooded the valley, glanced off the snow-patterned Alps above, and filled the meadows of grass and flowers with a brilliant green glow. Another July morning had come to Switzerland's only national park.

Our host, the superintendent, pulled into a parking space among some alpine larches. Except for an international highway through a distant portion of the park, the canton lets no cars come even near the park; so we strapped on our packs and walked for a mile up the mountain road to the entrance.

Climbing through coniferous forest resplendent with magenta rhododendron, we were at once enveloped in quiet, and knew that no sound or sight of automobiles would challenge the solitude. About a mile up the trail we met a group of foreign visitors who had collected a hatful of rare flowering plants, complete with roots. At each park entrance were signs (wordless but intelligible) prohibiting such practices, but for these visitors there had been too irresistible a temptation to take some of the park home with them. In most parks they might have been admonished and the matter forgotten. Not here. The superintendent promptly apprehended and lectured them, then levied a fine, payable on the spot. Though chastened, the visitors objected to a penalty for such a seemingly simple infraction. The superintendent pointed out that he was empowered by law to levy and collect twice as much. They paid.

Such enforcement, we observed, was more rigorous than any we had seen in two dozen countries, including our own. "Our people are proud of this park," the superintendent replied. "They will not permit it to be misused, not even once."

The Swiss have also adopted a rule the like of which we had not encountered in any national park: visitors must never leave the marked trails. We expressed surprise at this and submitted that such a policy curtailed freedom of men to roam as they willed. Precisely, was the reply. Men can roam else-

Sunrise over Heart Lake.

where; animals cannot. Men enter here on a strictly limited basis, disturbing the wildness as little as possible.

The Swiss National Park is also administered in part as an immense field laboratory in which research can be pursued for years. Here the chamois, ibex, red deer, and other animals have precedence over men, but after a long history of being hunted they are reluctant to move into areas inhabited by human beings. Wildlife is in some places rather difficult to see; we had to use a spotting scope to find a herd of ibex on a summit ridge and several deer on a steep green slope.

We lunched near a flower-strewn meadow, refreshed by breezes from the ice fields above. After that, we left; no one remains in the valley at night. It was one of the most enjoyable days of our lives— and we never once left the trail.

The more we reflected on these limitations the more the Swiss seemed ahead of their time. The park was established in 1914 with a view to leaving it to itself, free from adverse human influence, thereby enabling scientists to study gradual changes in plant and animal communities as the natural ecological balance restored itself. While aware that people must enter their park for refreshment and esthetic pleasure, the Swiss feel that visitors should also become aware of the fundamental principles of nature and conservation. The park has therefore been managed for more than fifty years on an ecological basis. Research is conducted under the auspices of the Swiss Academy of Sciences and the park is administered in association with the Swiss League of Nature Protection.

The Future of National Parks

Should the Swiss National Park be a model for Yellowstone? It is interesting to note that Yellowstone once had similar policies. There was a time when automobiles were strictly excluded from the park, when dogs and cats were prohibited, and drinking establishments were outlawed. No two parks, perhaps, can be administered exactly alike, but the Swiss National Park well illustrates the current international evolution of policy. It also provides insight into the query: what will the next century bring to national parks?

Nothing about the national parks is altering faster than policies regarding their use. So swiftly has the world taken up the principles of environmental conservation that it is not easy to predict what will happen to Yellowstone or any other park in the second hundred years of the national park idea. The emphasis in the past has been on preserving natural features and seeking economic benefits from tourism. Those efforts are expected to continue and be strengthened. Systems of national parks are likely to be established in countries still lacking them, and certain existing systems may be doubled and tripled in size as the benefits become apparent. The extraordinary interest in marine environments presages a rush to organize underwater parks, with the result that outstanding littoral, and perhaps even pelagic, ecosystems will be conserved.

The greatest breakthrough, however, in Yellowstone as well as elsewhere, may be the modification of man's influence and the development of sophisticated uses of the park. An important step toward understanding what parks may become is the defining of what a national park should be. Many definitions have been advanced, but the scope of parks is now so great that no simple answer serves. Yellowstone, of course, is no longer the only model on which to base a definition. Although it was the first large segment of public land to be set aside under the pioneer principles of national parks, it was not the first public land to be set aside for park purposes, nor the first to be identified in legislation as a "national park," nor was the United States first to set aside public parks. Since 1879 the national park idea has been promoted by an increasing number of countries and debated in international forums. From such forums we obtain a collective focus on national parks in modern society— and a definition that should satisfy most nations. For example, the International Union for the Conservation of Nature and Natural Resources (IUCN) in 1969 suggested a definition along the following lines.

National parks are places (1) where relatively large areas with one or several ecosystems are not materially altered by human exploitation and occupation; where plant and animal species and geomorphological sites and habitats are of special scientific, educational, and recreational interest; or where there are natural landscapes of great beauty; (2) where the highest competent authority of the country has taken steps to prevent or to eliminate as soon as possible exploitation or occupation in the whole area and to enforce effectively the respect of the ecological, geomorphological, or esthetic features that have led to its establishment; and (3) where visitors are allowed to enter, under special conditions, for inspirational, educational, cultural, and recreational purposes.

To eliminate too broad an application of the concept, the IUCN further recommended that governments not designate as national parks such places as: scientific reserves entered only by special permission; privately managed reserves without some type of recognition and control by the highest competent authority of the country; and heavily exploited areas of high density use where public outdoor recreation is the primary purpose and conservation of ecosystems subordinate to it.

This definition has little to do with the mission of national parks in the social affairs of varying cultures; that changes from country to country. Nor is it specific about how such parks are used. Nevertheless, from an accepted standard of what parks are, governments can better decide what policies to adopt and what management methods to follow.

Delicate Uses

If the national parks are to be conserved and used "in such manner and by such means as will leave them unimpaired for the enjoyment of future generations," we may expect certain alterations of current practices. Some of these alterations are being debated or actually tested; others have been in effect in some parks for a long time. In discussions of these matters not only with park officials in approximately thirty countries but with officials of continental and international organizations, the message for the future emerges complex but clear. It coincides with the 1886 recommendation to Congress to avoid the "vandalism of improvement." Or as Theodore Roosevelt said at Grand Canyon National Park in 1903: "Leave it as it is. You cannot improve on it. The ages have been at work on it, and man can only mar it."

Adoption of this policy would call for the gradual elimination of campgrounds, hotels, shops, gasoline stations, employee housing, museums, motorboats, air overflights, and even automobiles. The functions of federally operated campgrounds inside the park are gradually being replaced by privately operated campgrounds outside. Already the number of private campgrounds in the United States exceeds the number of federal, state, and municipal campgrounds combined. Not only does this eliminate the need for park rangers to "play nursemaid to campers," as a spokesman for private campground owners pointed out, but the private facilities provide more luxury than can be permitted inside national parks. Best of all, they do not pre-empt prime parkland.

Hotels, shops, and houses are all parts of an urban commercial complex better handled by private enterprise outside a park. A few national parks, such as Great Smoky Mountains and Haleakala in the United States, approach this design. Park museums, which the National Park Service has so splendidly pioneered, are introductory to park features and could be removed to peripheral sites. This would enhance the role of such discreet on-site interpretation as low-profile exhibits, self-guiding trails, limited-range broadcast transmitters, and, of course, the personal interpretive services offered by rangers and naturalists.

The arms of Yellowstone Lake have been closed to

Left: Hot stream in winter, near Madison Junction. *Above*: Steam over snow, Mammoth Hot Springs terraces.

all but hand-propelled craft, a policy that helps to maintain some of the original peace and quiet in those areas. There are people who say that horses could be retained in national parks, but only if trails are routed away from meadows, bogs, or slopes with easily erodable soil. Other wilderness devotees believe that horses have no place in national parks because of the damage they do to vegetation, especially in spring and summer, and because of the necessity of introducing exotic forage for them, although the latter could be prohibited by regulation. They say that long trail distances in Yellowstone are no longer a valid reason for preferring horseback over hiking trips, because with the new, lightweight equipment and freeze-dried foods there is little problem in back-packing burdensome supplies; long-distance hikers can still limit their packs to the usual thirty or forty pounds. If all this seems to rule out hiking on the part of the elderly, it should be kept in mind that a sixty-seven-year-old grandmother hiked the 2,000-mile-long Appalachian Trail two and a half times. Age is not necessarily a deterrent.

The greatest revolution in management of national parks may be the replacement of present systems of public transportation. Some people feel that automobiles and snowmobiles have little place in national parks. Even with engines that do not pollute the environment the question remains: how desirable is a park experience in which the driver of an auto meets 3,000 cars in an afternoon? In a large park like Yellowstone, some system of public transportation to replace private vehicles seems inevitable and indeed is already being tested in other parks. A shuttle bus system might be inaugurated, with passengers getting on and off at numerous designated stops. Or perhaps there could be a fleet of smaller vehicles that would operate like dolmus taxis of Turkey or publicos of Puerto Rico, which pick up passengers anywhere on a prescribed route. Either system would at least reduce the number of vehicles on park roads.

Some have advocated tramways as a solution to the transportation dilemma, but the destruction of scenery and wilderness atmosphere by such installations has been convincingly demonstrated in national parks of other countries; roads are much less ruinous to the landscape and, with proper design, less visible. Aerial tramway rides, like motorboats and hunting, can be enjoyed in other places. We have never heard a sufficient justification for cable cars in the national parks.

Voices of the Future

And yet, perhaps more important than the technological problems of introducing visitors into wild and scenic areas are the challenges of making their visits memorable, of even changing their lives. Any person who spends time in the management of national parks learns very early that the care of supposedly "undisturbed" areas is difficult, complex, and frequently vexing. Park rangers, naturalists, maintenance men, and administrators often work nights, weekends, and holidays and still do not meet all the demands. Buffeted by foe and sometimes by friend, they may eventually adopt a highly individualistic view of what a national park should be. They may also observe some heartwarming reactions to the park and its management, which restore their confidence and help reaffirm their respect for the wilderness. They themselves find in the park a renewal of life and spirit.

But there are different kinds of wilderness and different approaches to them. "In my opinion," said one park administrator, "defining an area as wilderness, even under the Wilderness Act, does not necessarily make it another Yellowstone National Park. Few parcels of land are managed as total ecological units like this one."

Yellowstone officials are loath to introduce into the wilderness anything that would alter or destroy its most delicate values. "I am certain," said a park naturalist, "that you cannot dump an infinite number of people into the back country without causing a disruption of the ecosystem, not to mention the esthetic values. If we encourage hundreds of thousands of people a year to go into the back country we would lose the very thing they want to see. I don't foresee that the whole of Yellowstone will be devoted to wilderness; there are too many things here that people ought to have an opportunity to see. But we may have to zone some areas in the park and say: 'No one goes in here; this is a prime grizzly-rearing area.'"

The wildness itself takes on an almost mystic significance the more these specialists learn about it. Freedom is the issue. In national parks men do not observe wild animals kept on display across a moat or watch them through iron bars, or toss out cookies in exchange for tricks. "When we see a wild bear doing nothing but grubbing in the ground or picking berries, or just passing through, it becomes an event," a ranger said. "We get a thrill out of knowing that that animal is free. This is an experience of a lifetime."

Visitors agree, and the question they most often ask is "Where are the bears?" But they usually refer to the well-known panhandler on the highway, and this disturbs biologists. "Our task," they say, "is to convey somehow that the roadside bear is hardly worth watching; he is captive to artificial feeding and you can see that in a zoo." Rangers are of the same mind. "We must stop this beggar," they say, "and put him totally back in his natural habitat. We also cannot tolerate that comedian injuring people along the road."

The problem of the flood of visitors concerns all park personnel. One naturalist advocates more day use and less overnight use of Yellowstone.

All visitors who remain overnight add to the pollution problems. They require more assistance to living—meals, showers, lodging, laundry—than those who come for a day-long visit, and require facilities that encroach upon park land. Even though we have nearly 3,500 square miles, there is just not room to accommodate all human beings who wish to remain overnight. Fortunately there

appears to be an increasing tendency for visitors to stay outside the park. The dilemma we face, however, is that if you decrease overnight use you increase the need for transportation into and out of the park.

Some rangers feel that certain facilities, such as roads, are not entirely injurious. "A piece of blacktop is not the worst thing in the world," says one. "It may save an area. It channelizes traffic and confines visitor activity. If the road avoids streams or wildlife feeding grounds, it does little damage to the resources. Lay roads lightly and sparingly on the land, in only small portions of the park, and you give many thousands of people a great experience without destroying wildlife." To this the superintendent adds: "We do not need roads everywhere, of course; that would be far more Yellowstone than visitors want. You can get scenic fatigue in this park."

Though they would take out most fixed facilities, experienced managers encourage such human uses as wilderness camping, cross-country skiing, and perhaps a few horseback trips, but only on a limited scale. A park official told us:

We have developed impact areas, with a great deal of public use, very close to points of interest, and as a result have damaged some highly fragile areas. People are upset about this, particularly in the Upper Geyser Basin. Generally, I think the public would like to see cars taken completely out of that basin. I like the theory I heard from New Zealanders: don't put a road or a parking area closer than thirty minutes' walk from any important feature. The more I think about that, the more I like it.

We have approached that sort of thing at Norris Geyser Basin, and people now have to walk quite a way to get from the parking lot to the points of interest; yet we have found that public attendance has increased. People are walking and enjoying it. As far as crippled visitors are concerned, I have seen paraplegics in wheelchairs tour the whole Upper Geyser Basin without any help. Age and infirmity have little or nothing to do with how this park is used. I have seen people as old as eighty-five walk those whole basins. They come in on bus tours, get up at 4:30 in the morning, and walk nearly all the trails before breakfast. They have a total appreciation for what they see because they are out by themselves.

There seems to be universal agreement that air should be free from noise as well as pollution. Happily the incidence of sonic booms has decreased, and park officials have eliminated such activities as loudspeaker talks that intruded upon the quiet of the geyser basins and motorboats that disturbed the wild-life and wilderness effect. Helicopter flights have been restricted to cases of emergency.

Just as pipelines, canals, jetports, and supersonic aircraft have been rejected elsewhere in modern society, so the Yellowstone staff is removing installations once deemed essential. "We have taken out more than 9,000 fourteen-inch-diameter guard posts from the roadside," the superintendent told us, "and have removed seven miles of guard rail in the park. In three years there have been no accidents on account of this. We mark our roads with only a single center stripe. Yet we have not had a single accident attributable to this. The solid line, like the absence of railings, requires a driver to use good judgment."

For all its trials at the hands of men, Yellowstone National Park has, in the words of its managers, survived the first hundred years with a minimum of damage. Furthermore, the park is believed to be capable of handling nearly 30,000 people a day without environmental degradation. "The troubles in the past were caused not by large numbers of people," said a park official, "but by us. Now we have learned."

We asked the superintendent what he regarded as the Number One problem of the day, and he was quick to reply:

Impact. We have to find out what this park can stand in the way of visitation. That is the major question which every park official must face, and the sooner it is answered the better. Planning and development must always be predicated upon what we believe to be the ceiling of visitor use.

What we have now is simply too many people trying to be on the same square foot of ground at the same time, and it doesn't work. There are ways of spreading use, but that is not the ultimate answer. You have to develop a level, an intensity of use first, and then say that everything else is subordinate. It is a hard decision, and maybe even difficult politically. But it has to be done. We must have the courage to adopt a limit, and when that is reached, the expansion of public use is halted.

Once this is done successfully, the management of a national park comes back to matters of wilderness use and maximum human enjoyment of the purposes for which the park was set aside. As a naturalist told us:

To me, the real enjoyment of this wild country requires considerable effort. Some people say that if you could fly in by helicopter and land in the midst of this wonderful territory, that would be great. But it wouldn't. I firmly believe that it takes a good deal of conditioning for a person to be able to appreciate the basic values of wilderness we are trying to conserve in this park. Anyone can experience them, regardless of age, affluence, color, race, or creed. But each man needs a period in which he prepares himself mentally and physically to get the most out of this environment. When he is prepared and "tuned in," then the best that this park has to offer is his. He can go out in a canoe, with his own strength and his own skills, camp along the shore of a lake or stream, hear the coyotes calling, see the stars through the clear air at night, and sleep like he never slept. That, to me, is tremendous.

1972–2072

These voices and hopes are part of a call for conservation that has gathered momentum rapidly in recent years. The high standards and strict limitations sought by the Yellowstone staff, and in a different way already applied by the Swiss, are reflected internationally in principles adopted by the United Nations. A national park, in order to qualify for inclusion on the UN List of National Parks and Equivalent Reserves, must have strict statutes for the protection of wildlife—no hunting, fishing, woodcutting, cultivation, animal-raising, or mining—and wardens to enforce the law. A park must be large enough—at least 5,000 acres—to be manageable as a self-sufficient unit, and it must have an adequate budget. Such a park can fulfill its mission to the highest degree.

And this mission? In conserving Yellowstone for a century, men have learned a great deal about how to administer and use a national park, and have found some clues on major uses to come. If present indications are correct, the park will serve its greatest purpose in an almost totally natural state, and one of its major missions will be to refresh the human mind and spirit. More people appear to be coming to sample the silence, the music of winds and waterfalls, the voices of mammals and birds. The value of solitude, with large amounts of open space, is likely to become so great that men will come with no more plan than to sit and think, or somehow to strengthen their identity with the land and their fellow creatures. Appreciation of wilderness values may reinforce efforts to control burgeoning human population or modify aggressive behavior. The national parks, as constants, will remind men of their original environments; by these habitats all others will be measured.

This being so, the parks are likely to be sustained as standards of environmental purity. Yellowstone, the progenitor, will need to excel in pure air, water, and landscape. Installation of pollution abatement devices is commendable but would be unnecessary if facilities were reduced. Already there is excellent progress in burying unsightly transmission lines. If some rangers had their way, the boardwalks in the geyser basins would be replaced by paths of equal safety but less offense to human sensibilities.

Logically, school education will continue to refine the public attitude toward natural ecosystems. Scientists will retrieve, analyze, and disseminate data about the habits of animals such as grizzly bears. As a result, greater numbers of people will be alert to the presence of healthy ecosystems in Yellowstone, regulated perhaps more scientifically than politically.

As all this comes to pass, park visitors will be able to indulge in what may become a major use: the enjoyment of moods. To talk of moods as one of the paramount resources of national parks seems trite in robust technological societies where development and conquest have been the principal motivations of human endeavor. But men are discovering, in the lesser-developed as well as the overdeveloped countries, that important values exist beyond the familiar ones of industrial and financial progress.

Frontiers of the Spirit

Thousands of persons come to Yellowstone each summer to hike or climb the peaks or descend into the canyons, getting away from even themselves, submerging into the forest moods. Some set up their easels and begin to paint. Photographers may take elaborate equipment into the back country. These people discover an unexpected confusion of worlds within worlds, so many that the summer itself would never be long enough to capture each color, each shadow, each light, each miniature miracle. Naturalists explore with tiny lenses some incredible scenes that others miss. Using tape equipment they catch and carry away recorded music of the wilderness. They take down conversations among coyotes, orchestrations of wind in pines, concertos of falling water, tympanic rolls of thunder.

For these people the coming of dawn to Yellowstone Lake has a special message. Their ears are receptive to the call of a gull passing over, their eyes to the colors on distant cliffs, their sense of feeling to the fresh, cool breezes. For some persons the best way to sample the exhilaration of wilderness life is a trip by canoe. They paddle along the shores of Shoshone Lake, for example, and see goldeneyes bobbing up and down around the boat, or a mink with a fish in its mouth loping along the shore, or river otters playing about, poking their heads out of the water here and there. Canoeists float offshore and watch the courting ritual of sandhill cranes: one jumps in the air and yodels, and then the other jumps. The next morning, from their camp at the edge of the lake, they watch the mists over the marsh and listen to the sounds of geese overhead and cranes in the wet meadows, or they laugh at a flock of young mergansers that run across the water and try to climb into the air, but cannot because they do not yet have flight feathers.

Poetry abounds in Yellowstone's moods. Who can read it all? We listen to whispers of life in the swirling clouds. Light bursts from the sculptured ebony of obsidian cliffs. Soft scents of mint rise out of the meadows and dissipate. When snow lies over the land, the tracks of animals are as punctuations of time, and nothing less than the signature of centuries.

Sometimes a man feels almost as though he were separated from the earth and going in a different direction, or had entered another dimension. Consider the case of a biologist who worked many years in Yellowstone, studied some of its major mysteries, and tried to determine the characteristics and functions of a part of the ecosystem. One summer evening a curious event occurred:

It wasn't the kind of thing I'd attribute to imagination. I'd been out for a week or so. I knew there were no other people for twenty miles in any direction. I was alone in the back country. This particular day I'd put in about forty miles on horseback and was returning to the Cold Creek patrol cabin when the sun was gold and slanting across the edge of the Mirror Plateau.

Maybe it was because I was tired, I don't know, but I had just come to the edge of the meadow when suddenly I had the strangest feeling of being out of place in time. I couldn't to this day tell you whether I thought I was back in time or forward. I did not know whether a period of the past had joined me, or whether I had suddenly jumped into the future. It made no sense.

Time-wise, nothing jibed. I had simply entered some other time plane. It was the strangest thing. I've never had it before or since. I've often been in places where I wondered if people had ever walked there before. But this wasn't wonder. It wasn't imagination. It was feeling. Time as I knew it had changed. For that brief period of crossing Cold Creek Meadow to the patrol cabin I was not of this era. Rangers I've talked to have had the same sort of feeling when they were working alone in the back country. Whether it is a product of physical tiredness or of knowing that no one else is in that part of the country, or a combination of both, I don't know.

There is something almost cosmic or metaphysical in that experience; it seems to have affected the innermost workings of the human thought processes. Perhaps a long experience in the wilderness had made the biologist supersensible. What happened was a feeling of exhilaration brought on not by anything artificial but by solitude, by the wilderness. One may wonder whether the next breakthrough in human perception will come from the cultivation of such experiences. In this sense the national parks are frontiers of the mind.

Already there are precedents of a sort in the laboratory, as for example with bio-feedback of alpha brain waves, which can create similar feelings of detachment and exhilaration. In the wilderness the same effect is sometimes initiated by nothing more than the sun slanting over a golden meadow. "All the senses are hushed and quieted, the nerves soothed, the soul steeped in the infinite beauty of the scene."

Gibbon Falls.

So said the Earl of Dunraven about an experience involving great elation on a drowsy afternoon during his 1874 travels in the Yellowstone country. "And in truth a man is so wrought upon, his nerves are so excited and at the same time so gently calmed, so many different chords are struck and vibrate together, that he scarcely knows what to do or how to analyse and appreciate his feelings."

The Ultimate Quality

Experiences with moods need not be abstract, but many end serendipitously, with a hiker, for example, pondering revelations he never expected. Much time may pass, however, before such possibilities are thoroughly examined or widely enjoyed. Not all men are adapted physically or emotionally to comprehend the values of wilderness, let alone make use of them to stimulate action or inspiration. Yet if we make only the same amount of progress, relatively speaking, in the next hundred years as we have in the past, Yellowstone and its kindred national parks should come to be focal points for expansion of human vision and perception. They are, after all, the remnants of a fundamental biological environment in which man evolved. The very roots and origins of his existence, his mentality, his make-up, lie in them. In the world at large he is always testing, it seems, to see how far he can escape from the bonds of his earthly biological beginnings. But there are limits. Apparently a man can take only so much industrial progress before he finds it necessary to return for a while to his original milieu, enter the forest, and take up a refreshingly different pace. This is not perhaps a conscious feeling among all men; some would go mad in the wilderness. But others find themselves involved so deeply with it that they are never the same again.

"Have you ever seen a flock of seventy trumpeter swans take off from the Yellowstone River?" a ranger asked us. "They get up and 'walk the water,' and then take flight. It is a thrill you never forget."

To sustain the quality of such experiences appears to be the primary challenge of the next hundred years of national parks, whether in Yellowstone or Switzerland or Zambia. How to do it and still admit millions of visitors is one of the leading unsolved questions of our time. Yet this basic contradiction is not necessarily an obstacle. Many millions of human beings may know the pleasures of national parks without penetrating very deeply into them, or without straying off the trails, as in the Swiss National Park. They can visit only a limited section and be satisfied; from a lookout can be seen nearly all of the wilderness they wish to see. Ninety-nine per cent of the park can be left in its natural state for wildlife and for people who would go in by foot, with the wind and rain in their faces, to explore the frontiers of the mind and perhaps be "out of place in time."

By hiking, canoeing, camping, photographing, painting, studying, contemplating, men will come to know much of the wild and of themselves. A man once stood at the edge of the Yellowstone River and watched an osprey dive into the water to pick up a trout ten feet away. Otters playing in Hayden Valley offer hours of laughter to a human observer. It is possible to watch a grizzly "landscaping" the river bottoms by tearing up great chunks of ground, or approaching a band of elk and pulling one of the animals down. "That is what this ecosystem is all about," the superintendent told us.

In the end it may be simply that contemplation will be the human use for which the national parks will be most valuable. Action and adventure may be a part of this, but ultimately the reorganization of a man's thoughts is so personal that the success of it, the renewal, the fresh enthusiasm for life, will affect him more than anything else. He may well become a better man in the society to which he returns. As the Rocky Mountain naturalist Enos Mills once said: "The supreme triumph of parks is humanity. . . . He who feels the spell of the wild, the rhythmic melody of falling water, the echoes among the crags, the bird songs, the wind in the pines, and the endless beat of wave upon the shore, is in tune with the universe, he will know what human brotherhood means."

Wildflowers near Mount Washburn.

12

When Winter Ends

The joy of living is his who has the heart to demand it.

THEODORE ROOSEVELT

March 14. Months have passed. Nothing seems as it was. No gentians bloom in the meadows now—there are no meadows, only flats of white. The rivulets that used to tumble over rocks and sound like harp glissandos are gone.

We look in vain for the warm, blue sky with drifting tufts of cumulus. Instead, the icy clouds fly over in fragments, leaping from ridge to ridge, skimming the peaks, dropping their showers of snow, dipping with fingers of fog into the dark and moody ravines. Through openings in the overcast we glimpse great streamers of snow swept by the wind from sharp mountain peaks and hurled out into the air. They spiral up into the sky, joining the marching fragments of cloud. Other snow-wraiths peel from cliffs and soar out over the valleys or vanish abruptly behind the crags.

This is not the Yellowstone we knew. That August world with its color and fresh aroma of growing plants has been gone for months. The Thorofare meadows and valleys, buried by snow, are more remote and inaccessible than ever. The elk we had seen on Big Game Ridge moved down into Jackson Hole for the winter. The deciduous trees, what few there were, turned color and lost their leaves. The shrubs did, too, and for most of the winter have shown no more than naked tips above the snow. All roses, orchids, and monkshoods withered away, their colorful, graceful forms replaced by lavish designs in crystals of ice. Nearly all of the ponds have not only frozen but disappeared under layers of snow.

We have returned, as we vowed, to see as much of Yellowstone as the snow permits. This time we approach from Montana, coming south through fleeting gales of snow. Past Electric Peak, whose summit is intermittently diffused by blowing snow, we climb to 6,000 feet and head east along the Yellowstone River.

Sun rays lance through the clouds and turn into flitting fountains of light. A valley gorge that was dark and gloomy a moment ago bursts into a soft, luminescent glow. The pines and firs take on outlines of light, in the way that clouds gain silver lin-

Winter storm over Swan Flat.

ings, and leap into three-dimensional profile. The pattern of steep forest slopes is that of herringbone, broken only where the wind whipped through and stripped the snow from groves of trees.

Along the rolling hills beside the Yellowstone River the wind fashions banks of snow into curving ridges, mounds, and overhanging cornices, sculpturing and polishing them to a silvery finish. Snowflakes whip into the woods and lose velocity, but not before they coat the windward half of every trunk with a layer of white. The sun reappears, seeming out of place in gales so cold. Light fills the darkest corners of dense coniferous groves, painting the shadowed snow on the forest floor with stippled designs and scattered squares, rectangles, and triangles. We see a lone elk out in the open, braced against the wind, scratching through the snow for forage.

We cannot remember how much time or how many valleys pass before we reach the Lamar River Valley. It, too, contrasts with the rich green world of last summer. At first glance we are almost shocked by the change, the lack of form, the absence of familiar landmarks. For miles ahead, the valley is flat and nearly unblemished, both sides bordered with rolling hills and the far end lost in a blaze of light scattered by the storm.

Whirlwinds of snow dance across the flats and hurl themselves into bordering thickets of pine. Two bison, gaunt from the winter's travail, stand forlornly at a patch of willow, looking as though they lacked the strength to swing their heads any more for a bite of buried sedge. Cottonwoods, naked and black, stand out as silhouettes against the white, marking the course of the river.

We turn to the east and head up Soda Butte Creek. Here and there the smothering ice and snow open briefly to reveal the water flowing beneath. Broad plates of ice and compacted snow have broken and fallen in the stream, looking like jumbled white ramps. On one open pond we see a pair of mallards and two handsome goldeneyes.

Before long we enter deep valleys of the Absaroka

A few Canada geese and other waterfowl remain in Yellowstone during the winter, occupying unfrozen portions of lakes and streams.

Above: Winds carry frozen steam
from thermal springs to nearby
branches, coating them with
rime and producing "ghost
trees." *Right*: Winter, Grand
Canyon of the Yellowstone
River. *Overleaf*: Snowscape
near the Lamar River Valley.

Range. The sheer cliffs of Barronette Peak on the left and Abiathar Peak on the right are no longer brown but almost entirely coated with snow, and great snowy cornices perch precariously, ready to avalanche. Where water has trickled over the ledges, frozen, thawed, and then refrozen, giant columns of translucent blue ice cling to the cliffs. Below them, most trees wear caps and robes of white, though their sagging limbs make them look like dancers with a hundred arms.

A patch of snow seems to detach and pull away from the cliff—but it is a magpie, flying out across the valley. Our eyes are carried up to another bird, much higher among the crags—a bald eagle. We are puzzled about its presence so far from an unfrozen river that might offer a catch of fish. Little else seems alive in the forest; the snow reaches eight feet deep as we come to the northeastern corner of the park.

The afternoon wanes rapidly on these short winter days, and we are compelled to return. The falling flakes become fewer as the stormy weather ebbs a bit. The wind abates and the land grows silent. Yet there should be some kind of sound in a world so famous for its animal life. We hear nothing, as though most of the animals for which this park is renowned had been buried or blown away by the storm.

Wildlife in Winter

March 15. Dawn breaks forth in gray, then blue, then gold. Moving out again toward the Lamar River Valley we pass Mount Everts, which looks at this hour like layers of crumpled white paper. Almost at once the abundance of life strikes our attention. The first light of dawn reveals silhouettes of elk on snow-covered ridges, as if the animals had come out from cover after the storm.

The sun climbs into a clear and cloudless sky and at once turns thousands of crystals of snow into glittering points of fire. Tufts of snow on the tips of pine needles melt and run down, clinging to the trees like strings of miniature lights. Blue shadows stretch out behind yellow clumps of grass that the wind kept free of snow.

We see more elk—not masses moving about like caribou in Canada but small bands here and there, some so distant that we find them only with binoculars. The animals are distributed over hilltops, slopes, bottomlands, rocky places, the edges of woods. As we locate their forms, which often blend with shadows or rhyolite outcrops, we begin to realize that an enormous population of wildlife does exist out there.

Some of the elk are standing. Some are eating. Some are lying down. A few appear to be sleeping. Evidence of them is everywhere: tracks and trails, shrubs chewed almost to stubs, whole hillsides trampled and compacted. All the animals appear to have a healthy coat of fur. A few of the males are "lopsided," their antlers having broken off, up to now, on one side only. If we are lucky we shall see a magpie perched on the back of an elk, picking off parasites.

Though elk are the most abundant ungulates in this blue-gold world, there are other inhabitants. As we approach a thicket of sagebrush, two dozen ravens fly up in a black cloud. They have been feasting on the carcass of an elk. At that moment we see a coyote which was also at work on the remains. We stop. The coyote raises its ears and moves its head from side to side. Consumed with curiosity it melts away in the sagebrush, slowly walks in a circle around us, comes to the carcass again, and, satisfied that no serious danger is near, resumes its meal.

We frequently sight small groups of bison. These animals walk with a heavy gait, most often around the frozen ponds where sedges may be found under the snow. For a good part of their day they also stand as in a stupor. Some may stand for hours beside a cliff from which radiant morning warmth reflects.

Farther on, we come to bighorn rams at rest on a yellow bank. A short way upslope other rams paw patches of snow that may conceal some forage they missed on earlier rounds.

We do not see any deer or pronghorn; they cannot compete with heavy snow at the higher elevations. We saw large herds of them at lower levels along the

Summer touches the alpine meadows near Dunraven Pass.

Yellowstone River, where the snow fell lightly yesterday or not at all.

Abundant tracks tell much of what went on last night. Across the rivers, down the roads, along the slopes, there are too many to count: trails of coyotes, moose, elk, deer, bison, red squirrel, snowshoe hare, and perhaps the rare red fox. Our ears catch voices of other inhabitants. While some sounds are muffled, the clear air transmits soft and delicate songs such as the plaintive whistle of the solitaire. From somewhere in the distance comes the rapping of a downy woodpecker, the nasal notes of a red-breasted nuthatch, and the music of a mountain chickadee.

This winter world of Yellowstone is not dead after all. Snow neither buries the spirit of Yellowstone nor conceals the workings of the living world. Natural functions continue, although some are dormant; we see no grizzly bears because it is too soon for them to emerge from their dens.

On our summer ride and hike through Thorofare country last year we had come upon too many things for human eyes to see, or brain to comprehend, at once. Now it is the same: patterns of snow dunes, circles drawn by swaying grass at the command of the wind, a lonely sage protected in a circle of conifers, red stems of willow, pines that sit in cups of snow from which the fallen flakes have blown away or melted. Where fragments of ice or snow fell away from trees and cliffs and rolled like snowballs down a concave slope, they left behind a trench; or they bounced along and etched dotted lines on the landscape. When President Theodore Roosevelt visited Yellowstone in the winter of 1903 he said: "I should like to point out that sometime people will surely awake to the fact that the Park has special beauties to be seen in winter; and any hardy man who can go through it in that season on skis will enjoy himself as he scarcely could elsewhere."

To Produce a Wolf

March 16. We are out on snowshoes today to explore beyond the roads. Clouds of steam herald geysers and hot springs, and we find that winter has had a negligible effect on the thermal features. However, the heat and steam play interesting tricks. In the midst of deep frozen drifts are patches of ground completely free of snow. These are a result of the rise of heat from subsurface circulating water and the consequent warming of the ground.

At first glimpse, hot emerald pools in the midst of a snowy landscape seem out of place. Nor do we associate winter with swirls of steam and colorful boiling cauldrons. Yet in a maze of white landscape are the same deep blues and greens and oranges that so fascinated us in summer. The heated waters are discharged as faithfully in winter as in any other season, but superheated steam in icy air produces clouds that billow as though from a volcano. Carried by breezes, the droplets of steam turn to crystals of ice, blow into the woods and collect on branches of trees, forming deposits of rime. So constant is the accumulation that trees in the path of the steam are coated in a ghostly white and are in fact called "ghost trees." Some bend to the ground under the collected weight of frozen steam. The forms are delicate and numerous; in some places it looks as though a waterfall had poured out of nowhere, covered the trees, then stopped.

There are other marvels of Yellowstone in winter: ground fog pierced by jets of steam, delicate layers of tiny columnar ice crystals caused by steam that escapes from the ground and freezes, insects laying their eggs near hot springs in January while inches away the temperature is below zero. In parts of the thermal basins there is almost a greenhouse climate, with plants growing beside the springs, and elk move down from the high country to take up winter residence there.

A week from now the vernal equinox occurs and in warmer climates people will say that spring has begun and they will look for signs of budding flowers and greening grass. Not here. It will be a month at least before the first sure signs of growth are evident. Masses of snow must melt and feed the streams until these change into roaring cascades. Sleeping wildlife will awaken and emerge. Pelicans will return from the south and take up nesting on the Molly Islands as they have for centuries. Elk will climb back into the highlands, and by the time the avens blooms on tundra summits, the process will have reached its peak.

Although visitors who come in summer miss most of this progression of spring, or the bugling of elk in autumn, or the white landscapes of winter, they will find in the woods more pleasures and revelations than they imagined: the delicate aroma of mint in lowland meadows, the tang of resin in lodgepole forests, the sight of coyotes loping across a sagebrush flat. They will discover Yellowstone's greatest secret—that most of its wonders are concealed only if we do not search for them. Understanding this, we may perhaps agree with Ralph Waldo Emerson that the mark of wisdom is to see the miraculous in the common.

Yet as a whole, Yellowstone does have miraculous aspects—not so much because of geysers and deep yellow canyons, but because of what the park itself may presage. Here man slowed his greed for land and his inhumanity to beast. Here he held up his hand in a protective gesture, not to sustain a commercially valuable animal population or to put wild beasts on public view, but to preserve an entire life system with its variations, its changes, its yet-undiscovered miracles. Significantly, he protected even predators such as the wolf, which was for a long time symbolic of wilderness hazards that had to be removed—and almost were.

Few men have reduced this matter to simpler, more meaningful terms than the eminent ecologist and humanist Sir Frank Fraser Darling. There is hope yet, he said, for a country that can produce a wolf.

Yellowstone is producing wolves again, and perhaps more than anything else that fact symbolizes the potential of the human species to mature, to be humane. If this spirit prevails in the future as widely as the spirit of aggression has in the past, a new and interesting age may come about.

Like some noble experiments of mankind, Yellowstone National Park survived its difficult years and emerged so strong, so universally popular, and so admired that the most powerful detractors could not seriously threaten it. The principle of the national park, which has spread to more than a hundred countries, is now a part of our culture.

Today, the experience of Yellowstone forms an initial part of a greater human experiment. In the national parks man is learning to preserve whole landscapes as sanctuaries for wildlife. If he succeeds, he may someday be able to make the earth itself a sanctuary for man.

Bibliography

General

Adams, Ansel and Newhall, Nancy, *The Tetons and the Yellowstone*, 1970, Five Associates, Redwood City, California.

Canter, Stanley G., *Winter Comes to Yellowstone*, 1969, Yellowstone Library and Museum Association, Yellowstone National Park, Wyoming.

Dasmann, Raymond F., *A Different Kind of Country*, 1968, The Macmillan Company, N.Y.

Harroy, Jean-Paul, *United Nations List of National Parks and Equivalent Reserves*, 1971, Hayez, Brussels, Belgium.

Ise, John, *Our National Park Policy*, 1961, Johns Hopkins Press, Baltimore.

Johnson, Paul C., *National Parks of the West*, 1965, Lane Magazine & Book Company, Menlo Park, California.

Lystrup, Herbert T., *Hamilton's Guide, Yellowstone National Park*, 1969, Hamilton Stores, Inc., West Yellowstone, Montana.

Muir, John, *Our National Parks*, 1901, published in 1970 by AMS Press, Inc., N.Y.

Sutton, Ann and Myron, *The American West: A Natural History*, 1969, Random House, N.Y.

Tilden, Freeman, *The National Parks*, 1968, Alfred A. Knopf, N.Y.

Geology

Allen, E. T., and Day, A. L., *Hot Springs of the Yellowstone National Park*, 1935, Carnegie Institution of Washington, D.C.

Keefer, William R., *Geologic Story of Yellowstone National Park*, 1972, Bulletin 1347, U.S. Geological Survey, Government Printing Office, Washington D.C.

Love, J. D., and Reed, John C., Jr., *Creation of the Teton Landscape*, 1968, Grand Teton Natural History Association, Grand Teton National Park, Wyoming.

Marler, George D., *The Story of Old Faithful*, 1969, Yellowstone Library and Museum Association, Yellowstone National Park, Wyoming.

Matthews, William H., III, *A Guide to the National Parks, Their Landscape and Geology*, 1968, The Natural History Press, Garden City, N.Y.

Wildlife

Banko, Winston E., *The Trumpeter Swan*, 1960, U.S. Bureau of Sport Fisheries and Wildlife, Government Printing Office, Washington, D.C.

Burt, William H., and Grossenheider, R. P., *A Field Guide to the Mammals*, Houghton Mifflin Company, Boston.

Diem, Kenneth L., *Banding Studies of Water Birds on the Molly Islands, Yellowstone Lake, Wyoming*, 1967, Yellowstone Library and Museum Association, Yellowstone National Park, Wyoming.

Harry, Bryan, and Dilley, Willard E., *Wildlife of Yellowstone and Grand Teton National Parks*, 1964, Wheelwright Lithographing Company, Salt Lake City, Utah.

Hubbard, Fran, *Animal Friends of Yellowstone*, 1970, The Awani Press, Fresno, California.

Peterson, Roger T., *A Field Guide to Western Birds*, 1961, Houghton Mifflin Company, Boston.

Schoonmaker, W. J., *The World of the Grizzly Bear*, 1968, J. B. Lippincott Company, Philadelphia.

Sharpe, F. Phillip, *Yellowstone Fish and Fishing*, 1970, Yellowstone Library and Museum Association, Yellowstone National Park, Wyoming.

Plants

Booth, W. E. and Wright, J. C., *Flora of Montana*, 1959, Montana State University, Bozeman.

Brock, Thomas D. and Louise, M., *Life in the Geyser Basins*, 1971, Yellowstone Library and Museum Association, Yellowstone National Park, Wyoming.

Craighead, John J., Craighead, Frank C., Jr., and Davis, Ray J., *A Field Guide to Rocky Mountain Wildflowers*, 1963, Houghton Mifflin Company, Boston.

Fowells, H. A., *Silvics of Forest Trees of the United States*, 1965, U.S. Department of Agriculture, Washington, D.C.

McDougall, W. B. and Baggley, Herma A., *Plants of Yellowstone National Park*, 1956, Yellowstone Library and Museum Association, Yellowstone National Park, Wyoming.

Taber, Richard D., *Coniferous Forests of the Northern Rocky Mountains*, 1969, University of Montana Foundation, Missoula.

History

Bartlett, Richard A., *Great Surveys of the American West*, 1962, University of Oklahoma Press, Norman.

Beal, Merrill D., *I Will Fight No More Forever*, 1963, University of Washington Press, Seattle.

Bonney, Orrin H. and Lorraine, *Battle Drums and Geysers*, 1970, The Swallow Press, Chicago.

Chittenden, Hiram M., *The Yellowstone National Park*, edited by Richard A. Bartlett, 1964, University of Oklahoma Press, Norman.

Cook, Charles W., Folsom, David E., and Peterson, William, *The Valley of the Upper Yellowstone*, edited by A. L. Haines, 1965, University of Oklahoma Press, Norman.

Crampton, Louis C., *Early History of Yellowstone National Park and Its Relationship to National Park Policy*, 1932, Government Printing Office, Washington, D.C.

Dunraven, Earl of, *The Great Divide: Travels in the Upper Yellowstone in the Summer of 1874*, 1876, published in 1967 by the University of Nebraska Press, Lincoln.

Mattes, Merrill J., *Colter's Hell and Jackson's Hole*, 1962, Yellowstone Library and Museum Association, Yellowstone National Park, Wyoming.

Russell, Osborne, *Journal of a Trapper*, edited by A. L. Haines, 1965, University of Nebraska Press, Lincoln.

Shankland, Robert, *Steve Mather of the National Parks*, 1970, Alfred A. Knopf, N.Y.

Strong, W. E., *Trip to the Yellowstone National Park in July, August & September, 1875*, 1968, University of Oklahoma Press, Norman.

Index

Asterisks indicate pages containing photographs.

ACKNOWLEDGMENTS AND CREDITS

The authors and publishers wish to thank the National Park Service, United States Department of the Interior, for assistance in the preparation of text and illustrations for this book. In particular, the Superintendent and staff of Yellowstone National Park contributed to the development of ideas and gathering of data, and participated in the review of both manuscript and illustrations at all stages of production. For technical review of specific chapters, gratitude is expressed to the Rocky Mountain Branch of the United States Geological Survey, and to the Bureau of Sport Fisheries and Wildlife, also in the Department of the Interior.

Of those field officials who contributed to the making of this book, the greatest share was borne by William W. Dunmire, Chief Park Naturalist of Yellowstone National Park. In cooperation with the Board of Directors of the Yellowstone Library and Museum Association, Mr. Dunmire provided data, ideas, guidance and review on a sustained program that covered more than two years. To him and his Board, the authors and publishers offer special thanks and gratitude. Superintendent Jack K. Anderson and Regional Director Fred Fagergren are due special credit for their backing of the project in its difficult early phases, and for guidance during production of the manuscript. The authors are grateful to Frank F. Kowski and Lemuel A. Garrison who over the years provided an abundance of information on the history, management, and wilderness philosophy of Yellowstone National Park. Michael and Larry Sutton gave splendid support during the intensive stages of field work. Among other persons to whom a debt of gratitude is hereby acknowledged are Rick T. Anderson, William L. Baker, William Barmore, Thomas D. Brock, Ted J. Bucknall, Stanley G. Canter, Glen Cole, Jack L. Dean, John R. Douglass, George L. Downing, Margaret B. Dupaix, Harold J. Estey, Aubrey L. Haines, John H. Hast, Cornelius W. Heine, William B. Hendrickson, Keith Hoofnagle, Jim L. Hotchkiss, Douglas B. Houston, George J. Johnson, Robert J. Jonas, Richard L. Lake, Mary M. Meagher, Leroy E. Mills, Alden L. Nash, Dan Nordgren, Fred M. Packard, Neil J. Reid, Robert E. Sellers, and Orthello L. Wallis.

In the national parks of other countries, the authors have been supplied with information and guided by many persons. The list is so long that not all such assistance can be acknowledged in the space available here. However, the authors wish to thank particularly the following: Argentina: Andrés Biaggini, Maria Buchinger, Hugo Correa Luna, Italo Costantino, Benjamin Cozzi, Juan Daciuk, Lucio Debenedetti, Milan Dimitri, Ricardo Luti and Alberto Mendonça-Paz; Australia: Clif Bell, N. C. Gare, Keith Jarrott, D. F. McMichael, L. H. Smith, Howard Stanley; Bolivia: Percy Baptista, Rene Prieto Chacon, Elias Salame; Botswana: L. D. Tennant, Alexander Colin Campbell; Brazil: Alceo Magnanini, Harold E. Strang; Canada: Steve Kun, John I. Nicol, Keith Plowman, Alex Reeve; Colombia: Enrique Perez Arbelaez, Arturo Delgado Flores, Simon Max Franky, Teobaldo Mozo Morron, Antonio Olivares, Hernando Reyes-Duarte; Congo Republic: Paul Pierret; Costa Rica: Mario Boza, Kenton Miller; Dominican Republic: Angel Miolán; Ecuador: Juan Black, Cristobal Bonifaz, Peter Kramer, Enrique Laso Gonzales, Angel Lovato, Pablo Rosero, Oswaldo Vivanco; Guatemala: Jorge A. Ibarra; Italy: Vittorio Agnelli; New Zealand: Mervyn Burke, Ray Cleland, N. C. Coad, P. H. C. Lucas, John Mazey, V. P. McGlone, Gordon Nicholls, Walter Ollivier; Panama: Alfredo Castillero, Ricardo Gutierrez, Dario Tovar; South Africa: John T. G. Page; Switzerland: Robert Schloeth; Thailand: Dusit Banijbatana, Chalermchai Charuvastr, Boonsong Lekagul; Turkey: Özdoğan Aktar, Zekai Bayer, Suleyman Cakal, Orhan Camci, Necat Gülgün, Hugh Miller, Mahmut Molu, John Moseley, Paul F. Spangle, Lynn Spaulding; Venezuela: José Rafael Garcia, Edgardo Mondolfi, José Ramon Orta. In addition, special appreciation is paid to the Latin American Committee on National Parks, the Charles Darwin Foundation for the Galápagos Isles, the Organization of American States, the Food and Agricultural Organization of the United Nations, the Agency for International Development, and the International Union for the Conservation of Nature and Natural Resources.

To His Royal Highness, Prince Philip, the Duke of Edinburgh, and to Sir Frank Fraser Darling, Vice President of the Conservation Foundation of Washington, D.C., go our profound gratitude for their contributions to this work.

Ann and Myron Sutton

All photographs are by Charles Steinhacker except where otherwise noted. Credits read from top to bottom and from left to right.

Page 6, Bryan Harry; 18–19, Ernst Peterson; 22–23, Noel Ary; 23, Stanley Canter; 26, Ann and Myron Sutton; 30–31, 36–37, William W. Dunmire, 37, Harry Engels; 40, R. Ames: Photophile; 43, William W. Bacon III; 46, R. Ames: Photophile, Robert G. Johnsson; 47, William W. Bacon III; 48–49, Bryan Harry: 50–51, George Downing; 57, Hans W. Silvester: Bavaria Verlag; 58–59, Bryan Harry; 62–63, Josef Muench; 66 (bottom), George T. Morrison; 90, Harry Engels; 92, Stanley Canter; 97, Bill Ratcliffe; 103, 107, William W. Dunmire; 113, 114, Bryan Harry; 120–121, Hans W. Silvester: Bavaria Verlag; 131 (middle and bottom), William W. Bacon III; 135, National Archives; 137, 139 (top), Courtesy Yellowstone National Park; 139 (middle and bottom), 140, 145, National Archives; 146, Courtesy Yellowstone National Park; 147, Haynes Foundation, National Archives; 149, Haynes Foundation; 151, National Archives; 153 (top), Haynes Foundation; 153 (bottom), 155–157, Courtesy Yellowstone National Park; 158, Haynes Foundation, Library of Congress; 159, Courtesy Yellowstone National Park; 163, Haynes Foundation; 164–165, Courtesy Yellowstone National Park; 168–169, Library of Congress; 169 (bottom), Haynes Foundation; 170, Library of Congress, National Archives; 171, Courtesy Yellowstone National Park, Library of Congress; 173, Courtesy Yellowstone National Park; 175, L. McIntyre: Alpha Photos; 178–179, Ann and Myron Sutton; 181, Clem Haagner; 182, 185, Ann and Myron Sutton; 189, Freelance Photographers Guild; 195, Thea Thompson; 212, William W. Bacon III.

This book was planned and produced by Paul Steiner and the staff of Chanticleer Press.

Editor: Milton Rugoff

Associate Editor: Joanne Shapiro

Art Director: Ulrich Ruchti, assisted by Elaine Jones

Production: Gudrun Buettner, assisted by Helga Lose

Printed by Amilcare Pizzi, S.p.A., Milan, Italy

NORTH ENTRANCE

Gardiner

Electric Peak

MONTANA
WYOMING

**Mammoth
Hot Springs**

GALLATIN

RANGE

Gardner River

Mt. Holmes

Obsidian Cliff

Roaring
Mountain

Tow

Dunraven Pas

Hebgen
Lake

Cougar Creek

*Norris Geyser
Basin*

Norris

Inspiration Poi

West
Yellowstone

CENTRAL

Canyon

Yellowstone Falls

Artist Poi

WEST
ENTRANCE

Madison   River

Gibbon River

Madison

Firehole River

PLATEAU

HAY
VAL

MADISON

*LOWER GEYSER
BASIN*

IDAHO MONTANA
WYOMING

PLATEAU

*MIDWAY GEYSER
BASIN*

*UPPER GEYSER
BASIN*

*BLACK SAND
BASIN*

Old Faithful Geyser

Old Faithful

West Thu

*WEST THUMB
GEYSER BASIN*

Boundary Creek

SHOSHONE GEYSER BASIN

Shoshone Lake

**Grant
Village**

Lewis
Lake

Mt. Sheridan

PITCHSTONE

PLATEAU

Lewis River

Bechler

Beula
Lake   Hering Lake

Snake

Falls   River

SOUTH ENTRANCE